PARENTS
AND THE
SCHOOLS

PARENTS
AND THE
SCHOOLS

How to Insure Your Child's Academic Success... and Much More

Bill Pelaia

authorHOUSE®

AuthorHouse™
1663 Liberty Drive
Bloomington, IN 47403
www.authorhouse.com
Phone: 1-800-839-8640

First published by AuthorHouse   10/20/2011

ISBN: 978-1-4670-6290-9 (sc)
ISBN: 978-1-4670-6289-3 (ebk)

Library of Congress Control Number: 2011918637

Printed in the United States of America

Any people depicted in stock imagery provided by Thinkstock are models, and such images are being used for illustrative purposes only.
Certain stock imagery © Thinkstock.

This book is printed on acid-free paper.

This Record of Educational Progress is for:

_____

Acknowledgements

"Parents and the Schools" is based on the research and writings of Nancy Reckinger. Dr. Reckinger was Professor of Education and Human Growth and Development at California State University, Fullerton. For twenty years she was a teacher and counselor in public schools where she developed programs to meet the needs of gifted and underachieving students. Dr. Reckinger passed away in 2009, however, her influence upon children and schools will continue in this book.

To make this book consistent with proven successful practice, the Hollis Team at Stetson University, Deland, Florida, reviewed the information, paying particular attention to sections dealing with their areas of expertise. To my former colleagues I offer my gratitude for their contributions to this book.

The members of The Hollis Team:

Elizabeth (Bette) Heins, Ph.D. Nina B. Hollis Professor; Endowed Chair
Educational reform, exceptional student education, educational psychology, collaborative inclusion models, professional development schools, single-gender education, classroom management.

- Kathy Jo Piechura-Couture, Ph.D. Professor
Educational reform, exceptional student education, technology, professional development schools, collaborative inclusion models and curriculum for children with behavioral disorders, single-gender education, program assessment models and technology integration.

- Mercedes Tichenor, Ed.D. Professor
Educational reform, elementary education, curriculum and instruction, teacher professionalism, family and school connections, single-gender education, mathematics pedagogy.

- Debra Touchton, Ph.D. Associate Professor
Educational leadership, school reform, women in leadership, professional development schools.

- Douglas MacIsaac, Ed.S., Assistant Professor
Professional development schools, educational reform, teacher induction and mentoring, curriculum and instruction, single-gender education and gender based learning.

Address inquiries and suggestions to:
Bill Pelaia
bill.pelaia@celebration.fl.us

Introduction

"Parents and the Schools" is a program to help parents prepare their children for nursery school or kindergarten and make the most of their schooling through grade 12. However, parents can begin using this booklet at any grade level. It's never too late to make the most of school.

In order for children to be as successful as possible in school, parents need to be actively involved and stay involved in their children's learning. Many studies show that what the parents do is more important to a child's success than how much education the parents have or how much they make.

This book includes an overview of the way children develop and learn. The Educational Record Pages give parents a means of recording their child's progress from pre-school through high school graduation. It is aimed at **preventing problems** and making the time parents spend with their children as meaningful as possible. It has been tested and received the approval of educators and parents.

The use of this program fosters the kind of cooperation between home and school that educators desire and welcome. If schools receive children who are well prepared every year, everyone in the educative process benefits, particularly the child.

Welcome to the faculty.

Bill Pelaia

TABLE OF CONTENTS

Part I
Framework for Growing
And Learning

Introduction

The best interests of the child shall be the guiding principle
of those responsible for his education and guidance;
and that responsibility lies in the first place with his parents.

-The United Nations,
Declaration of the Rights of the Child

Congratulations! You have taken an important first step in making the most of your child's education.

The material contained in this manual will help you guide the education of children between the ages of 2 and 18. Ideally, you will begin using this manual when your child is 2, 3, or 4. The earlier you begin, the easier it is to develop good habits and build strong foundations.

If your child is in grade school, this material can help you check on progress, correct directions and support the strengths of your child. If your child is an adolescent, there is still time for you to check on basic reading and arithmetic skills, avoid conflict, and help with goal setting.

This manual appeals to parents of all children, because it is aimed at *preventing difficulties* and at making the time you spend with your child quality time. Parents whose children are gifted or who have difficulty with the learning process, will find this material especially helpful.

Objectives of this manual

The objectives of this manual are:

1. to produce a record of your child's progress,
2. to make you fully aware of his or her accomplishments,
3. to enable you to discover where your help is needed, and
4. to foster cooperation between home and school.

The information presented in this book helps you look at each child as a unique blend of capabilities to be nurtured and cultivated; then it helps you develop the potential you see.

1

Why this manual is needed

Human beings have few instincts. They have to learn practically everything, including parenting, and there are not many places in our society where people are helped with parenting skills.

Parents need to know what constitutes good development; what their children's abilities are; what school learning tasks are by grade level; and how to work with the school so their children have the opportunity to learn school tasks and to feel good about doing so.

Parents hire teachers to help *them teach their children* (although that basic concept is sometimes forgotten). Parents have both the right and the responsibility to participate actively and **knowledgeably** in the teaching partnership. If you believe in democracy, you also have the responsibility to teach your child how to participate in the partnership. Some parents have chosen to teach their children at home without hiring teachers, taking on the whole job. These parents have an even greater need to know what is involved and where they are headed. This manual salutes and supports all parents who are interested in actively participating in their children's education.

How this material will help you

You will be introduced to a brief overview of human development and a guide to helping your child. It points the way and tells you what to look for; at what ages children begin developing particular skills, when to intervene, and when to get help. It gives you a way to keep a record of your child's unique development, and valuable history, useful every time you move and also when your child is making important educational decisions, such as what subject field to concentrate on.

Unique material contained in this book

Special features of the material include:

1. Showing you how to discover and cultivate your child's qualities and to be sure the education provided meets your child's need.
2. Reading and arithmetic skill hierarchies, so that you, the parent, can determine with considerable accuracy how well your child knows the basic skills. You will also find out how to help if help is needed.
3. Educational Records, which you keep so that you are the continuing link between your child and the school.
4. Yearly Educational Checkups, which are just as important as dental and medical checkups.
5. Pages 101 through 115 provides suggestions for how to hold on to all those important school records and your child's annual school pictures.

There is no *one* right way or *one* right time for all children to learn. But you have the right and the responsibility to help your child find *a* right way and a right time. "Parents and the Schools" will **insure** your child's success in school and beyond.

All grade level and age related charts in this book are based on research and observations, however, as stated many times, every child is unique. In addition, the curriculum may differ from school to school. Make adjustments to these charts based on the needs of your child and the grade expectations of the school.

How to Insure Your Child's Success in School

Successful students have the following three attributes: (1) *high self-esteem;* (2) *sense of control* (they feel their actions and decisions make a difference in their lives); and (3) *interest in learning.* This book is designed to help you help your child develop these characteristics from their earliest years through high school. Your child will develop these attributes most easily when there is a three-way partnership of child, parent(s), and teachers.

You know more than anyone else about how your child learns, acts, and reacts. No one is as interested or spends as much time interacting with a child as the parents. Trust what you know about your child as you continue learning. To remain an active partner during your child's school years, you will want to learn as much as you can about child development so you can assist your child in developing *a high self-esteem*, *sense of control*, and an *interest in learning*.

Using the Manual

The book is comprised of six sections. Part I provides information for growing and learning and advises that you begin *Yearly Education Checkups.* Part II deals with the first five years; Part III with elementary school years; and Part IV with secondary years. There is a Developmental Record page for each grade. Part V contains a Guide to the Internet, Computer Use suggestions, how to avoid "The Summer Brain Drain", Resources, State Academic Standards, and References. Educational Record Pages, pre-school to grade 12, are in Section VI.

No matter your child's age, read Part I carefully. Next, move to your child's age section and become familiar with the developmental tasks appropriate for that age range. This will provide information to determine your child's stage of development. Then go back and fill in as much of the earlier years as you can.

You won't be able to follow all of the suggestions in this book, nor is it expected. The intent of this book is to help you recognize the unique abilities and capacities of your child, value the uniqueness, and help you provide the nurturing needed for your child's development, both at home and school. This is your book. Use whatever is helpful to you and your child, pass up the rest, and don't let it bother you.

Understanding Your Child

Everyone knows that plants are not all alike. We understand that roses need sun, azaleas need shade, and trees need lots of room to grow. Children also have varied needs. If you 1) recognize the kind of person your child is, 2) cultivate strengths, and 3) communicate that you treasure this special person, your child will develop high self-esteem, the first key to success in school. If you pay attention to your child's efforts at self-direction, your child will develop a sense of control, the second key. Connecting the love of learning to your child's interests and purposes will develop the third key. Provide the three keys to school success and watch your child blossom.

Stages of Development

Material included in this book is drawn from theories of various experts. This chart gives an overview of the steps that lead to healthy development. References for further reading are located at the end of the manual.

Developmental Stages of Youth	Physical Development	Erickson's Psychosocial Developmental Tasks
Infancy 0-2 Years	Sits, stands, creeps. Stands. Walks alone. Hand preference emerges (18-24 months).	*Trust* 0-1.5 years Begins to form an identity if caretaker is dependable, warm, and fairly consistent. Otherwise *mistrust* develops.
Toddlerhood 2-4 Years	Rapid growth. More eye-hand coordination.	*Autonomy* 1.5-3 years Develops an independent spirit if given some freedom, allowed to test and assert self; needs to have some say in decisions. Need for parents to balance freedom and control. Otherwise *doubt* will develop.
Early Childhood 3-6 Years	Girls ahead of boys in physical development and large muscle development. Increase in speed and coordination. Need independence for physical activity.	*Initiative* Plans and does things alone. Needs opportunities to be active, ask questions, and fantasize. Otherwise *guilt* develops.
Middle Childhood 6-12 Years	Girls still ahead of boys in physical development and in both large and small muscle development. Increasing skills with tools. High energy level-need for physical activity. Girls begin adolescent growth spurt toward end of this period.	*Industry* Seeks sense of accomplishment. Makes or builds things. Play becomes productive and the product is important to self-esteem. Needs to be successful often, especially at school. Finds pleasure in accomplishing tasks. Self-esteem destroyed by being inadequate frequently. Needs tasks and challenges within capacity. Otherwise *inferiority* results.
Adolescence 12-18 Years	Boys begin growth spurt. Adolescent growth spurt. Onset of sexual maturity— struggling to learn socially approved behavior.	*Identity* All previous stages blend into a unified whole so there is ego identity. Roles and experiences blend together so person establishes a knowledge of who they are and where they fit in.

Stages of Development

Piaget's Cognitive Development Stages	Kohlberg's Moral Development Stages	Maslow's Hierarchy of Needs
0-2 Years *Sensorimotor Stage* Learning directed to simple skills—sucking, blowing, grasping objects, and reflex actions	Years *I. Obedience and Punishment Stage* Needs love, warmth, cuddling, and firmness. Cannot understand reasons. Copies parents	**These stages are not necessarily age-related, but are listed in their priority.**
2-4 Years *Preconceptual Stage* Symbolic ability—child can create a mental image of objects not present. Fantasy and reality are mixed. Insists that all objects are alive. Begins to relate experiences in sequence.	**4-9 Years** *Rewards Stage* Follows rules to gain some reward. Thinks parents are great—imitates them. Develops a sense of fairness. Needs to have positive behavior praised. Can begin to understand concepts such as honesty, truthfulness, etc.	**In other words, a person who is hungry is usually not thinking of anything else but food, but once full, goes on to the next step.**
4-7 Years *Intuitive Stage* Increased attention span. Groups objects by use or nearness. Gives thought to decisions.	**9-15 Years** *Approval-Duty Stage* Follows rules to win praise and approval. Sense of duty. Strong sense of fair play; expects to follow the rules and expects others to do so. Imitates people he/she feels strongly about. *Law and Order Stage* Adopts rules as his/her own. Respects authority and society. Needs to know the limits. Identifies with society, church, and school. *(sometimes skipped in this stage)* Questions society's values. Rebels against hypocrisy.	*Physical—* (Food, shelter, sleep) *Safety* *Security* *Belongingness* *Love* (by others) *Self-esteem*
7-11 Years *Concrete Operations Stage* Begins to reason logically about objects. Develops understanding of cause and effect. Concentrates longer. Understands how groups of objects are alike.	**16 Years and older** *Social Contract Stage* Careful not to violate the rights of others. Selecting personal and moral principles. Testing and thinking about morals. Needs to know what family rules and values are not negotiable. Needs to be able to discuss puzzling matters. *Moral Principle Stage* Upholds behavior that respects the dignity of life. Has a true conscience.	*Self-actualization* (developing capacities to be all one is capable of being)

12+ Years Abstract Thinking Stage Develops independent, critical thinking. Solves problems. Considers a number of possible answers. Uses abstract words with understanding. Considers long range goals and the past, present and future. Can plan. Concerned with the future, the ideal, the abstract, the remote.		

A Yearly Educational Check-Up
Is Good For Your Child's Health

Nothing is more important to your child's success than a Yearly Educational Checkup. The checkup takes time and effort, but it is quality time and effort well spent. You communicate your affirmation, respect, and support for your child. Children have a constantly developing power to participate in the decisions that affect their lives, especially if that power is not stifled. If you want them to make good life decisions, start early helping them learn how to do so. Include them as early as possible in every decision that affects them; this in itself helps develop the three characteristics needed for success. Make the checkup a regular yearly routine.

The first goal of each checkup is for you and your child to understand where your child is developmentally. Understanding means that you try to be sure you understand how your child sees the situation. A parent is frequently not looking at the same things the child is experiencing, much less reaching the same conclusions. The checkup times become easier with practice and are valuable for all of you. The more openly and honestly you talk with your child, the more you will learn, and the more you can help. Making your child feel special by emphasizing the year's accomplishments is always positive.

The second goal is to create a plan for what each person is doing to help development continue. In the early days, the plan is all yours. When your child starts school, it will be up to you to work with the many teachers who will join your team over the years to help them meet your child's individual needs. Gradually your child will want to participate, until one day he or she takes over the plan independently.

Steps to Take

Have a quiet, private session with your child. Make it fun, warm, encouraging and supportive.

Go over "Self-Esteem, pages 11 through 14. Are basic needs being met? If your child is old enough to understand the questions, go through them. If not, relate the questions to your child's behavior. Talk about the ideas on the list in words your child understands. Discuss your child's feelings. List things on your plan that you will do to provide esteem-building opportunities.

Read "Sense of Control", pages 15 and 16. Identify times you are letting your child make choices. Discuss the topic together. Would your child like to make more decisions? Where can you provide more opportunities? Add them to your plan.

Refer to "Motivation", pages 17 through 19. What are the motivators in your child's life now? How are you building on them? What may be stifling them? Who needs to do what to support them? Add these activities to appropriate plans—yours, your child's or perhaps the teachers'. Is outside motivation needed? What kind works best? Add to your plan if needed.

Check the stages of "Moral Development", pages 20 and 21. Listen to what your child says about values. Remember, your actions speak more loudly than words. You want to know what values your child is operating on. You may have to add items to your plan. Try to devise activities that will expose your child to moral reasoning at the next higher level of development.

Add anything new to the "Physical Developmental Record", page 26. If there is something that needs to be followed up, add it to your plan. Go over the Developmental Tasks for your child's age. Check the lists of tasks each year and decide which ones you will focus on in the future. From school age on, you will need to work with teachers.

Go over the Developmental Tasks for your child's age group. Check the list of tasks each year and decide which ones you will pursue. From school age on, you will work with teachers on mutually established goals and objectives. Refer to page 38 for information about how to do this part of the check-up.

Self-esteem: Is Your Child a Winner?

Self-esteem is what you think of yourself. You have high self-esteem if you feel you do many things well and the important things at least well enough. Low self-esteem is feeling you do not do things well enough, that you are not OK.

High self-esteem is one of the three keys to success in school and parents have a great deal to do with the way a child's self-esteem develops. Decisions about who and what we are, will be made very early in life. You help the development of high self-esteem when you see your child as a winner, when you focus on abilities, strengths, and successes.

The Self-Fulfilling Prophecy

Perhaps the most important idea in the field of human development is the "self-fulfilling prophecy." It says that when parents and teachers believe their children are winners, they treat them like winners, and the children become winners. That means that adults treat children whom they see as winners differently than they treat other children. They encourage and help. They expect more, trust more, praise more, and respect and allow children to do more for themselves, make more decisions, try more things, and assume more responsibility.

Children need success experiences. If they have enough of them, they will overcome failures without giving up. Walking is a good example of how you help your child be successful. Even though walking is difficult, it has to be learned. All children fall down a lot when learning to walk—which could lead to a sense of failure. When parents support, encourage and praise enough at each small step, children continue to try and eventually learn to walk successfully.

With each success and failure, a person makes choices about future efforts. Failures often cause whole areas of experience to be discarded, as the person forever after says, "I'm no good at that." The personality hardens and limits its own life choices.

Abraham Maslow developed a psychology of "becoming all you can be." He claimed that each of us has two kinds of needs that we spend our lives trying to fulfill. The first is basic needs—food, sleep, and shelter. The second is growth needs—continuous learning. If basic needs are not met, most people cannot (do not have the ability to) pay attention to growth needs. So before all else, check your child's *basic needs:* physical wellbeing (food, sleep), safety and security, love and belongingness, esteem by others, self-esteem. Don't expect school success when a child is physically uncomfortable and/or does not feel capable of doing what is expected.

When basic needs are met, people feel the need to develop their capacities and talents. Growth is personally rewarding and exciting, even when it is difficult. People who are functioning at the appropriate growth level feel strong, sure of themselves, in control, full

11

of joy and happiness. These feelings of self-esteem are felt even when the job they are working on is hard and they are falling down a lot, as when learning to walk.

To help your child with self-esteem:

- Provide safety while encouraging risk
- Provide the security of rules and limits
- Encourage curiosity
- Allow choices
- Allow errors (falling down)
- Make a fuss over brave accomplishments (as you did over your child's first steps)
- Answer and ask questions
- Love and show it

Developing Self-esteem: A Checklist for Your Child

Listen carefully from the earliest years to the way your child answers the following statements (you may have to use different words with younger children). Make a list of answers as a part of every Yearly Educational Checkup. Discuss the answers together and record the way your child completes the statement beginning, "I like myself because . . . .". Aim for an increasingly longer list each year. Keep lists with the yearly Developmental Record page.

If you hear strong negatives, consider them loud warning signals. Make it your number one responsibility to create opportunities for child to 1) decrease the number of times your child feels inadequate and 2) increase the number of successes. Set goals your child can reach. If the problem is school related, ask for a plan that provides more academic successes. If a year's checkup is very negative, start keeping track of successes and encourage your child to do the same.

Help your child learn to replace outer adult control with personal self-control. Help your child learn self-discipline and to assume personal responsibility. With your child, discuss the pros and cons of choice and the responsibilities that come with the choice made. These discussions will help your child develop the understanding upon which self-esteem grows. Respond generously to requests for love and protection as well as for respect and self-control.

How to Use the Checklist

You may read the following to your child before you discus the statements. You can alter this based on the age of your child.

"Answer the following statements with "yes", "no", or "sometimes." "Yes" answers mean you feel like this most of the time and feel pretty good about yourself. "Sometimes" means you feel like this sometimes and are in the middle." "No" answers mean you hardly ever feel like this, and it may hurt to say so. Try to talk about why you said "no" and how you feel about it. Can you think of anything you can do to change it? Can you think of anything we can do or your teacher(s) can do to change it? If so, talk to us about it."

Personal Statements

1. I am OK. There are not very many things I would change about myself.
2. I feel confident most of the time.
3. I understand myself.
4. I can't think of anyone else I would rather be with.
5. I enjoy my own company. I am not lonely.
6. The people who count understand me. (Who are they?)
7. Growing up is an exciting adventure.
8. I can do a lot of things well, such as (name as many as possible).
9. People can usually depend on me.

10. I feel comfortable talking when I have something to say.
11. I enjoy learning things. (What things?)
12. I know how to get along with people who think differently than I do.
13. I am pretty sure of myself.
14. I am easy to like.
15. My parent(s) and I have a lot of fun together.
16. I usually make up my mind easily.
17. I get along OK with most people my age.
18. I am usually pretty happy.
19. Usually I am glad to be me.
20. I am as good looking as most people.
21. People at home pay attention to me.
22. I feel pretty successful.
23. Failing at something doesn't bother me a lot.

School Related Statements

24. I am doing as well as I can in school. (How well is that?)
25. My teachers like me.
26. Students in my class listen to me when I talk.
27. Teachers pay attention to me.
28. I think I do OK in my school work.
29. I am proud of my school work.
30. I like to be called on in class.
31. I am liked by most of the students in my class(es).
32. I have school pretty well figured out.
33. Most teachers understand me.
34. I know how to plan and pace my school work.
35. I enjoy most of school.
36. I am doing as well in school as I want to.
37. Being reprimanded at school doesn't bother me a lot.
38. I am pretty successful at school.
39. Teachers usually consider my feelings.
40. Sometimes I decide not to do what my friends are planning to do.

A Sense of Self Control:
Is Your Child Helping to Drive or Being Driven

People who have a sense of internal control believe that they have some control of what happens to them. Fate, luck, birth, the economy, or world affairs may affect their chances, but they still can do something to turn lemons into lemonade. These people believe that studying will raise their chances of passing the test; preparing for the interview will help them get the job; and figuring out the stock market will enable them to make money.

On the other hand, people who do not have a sense of external control believe that nothing they can do makes any difference. Luck, fate, or the system determines what will happen to them; it is out of their hands. They will pass the test, get the job, or win at the races if some outside force allows it to happen.

Since self control is one of the keys to success in school, a sense of internal control is worth nurturing.

Development begins early in life around the age of 2. Eric Erickson's developmental task at that age is autonomy, expressed as, "Me do it" or "I want to do it myself." When parents let their child do it or they help them do it themselves, the child develops an internal control system—self control.

Learning Cause and Effect

By adolescence, children who are allowed to have some control over their lives and to make some of their own choices develop an understanding of cause and effect through reasoning and reflecting about their choices. They need many of the following kinds of reasoning and reflecting experiences:

1. "I studied for the test and passed it this week; last week I goofed off and didn't pass it. By studying I can pass." If the work is so hard that no amount of studying helps them pass, children decide that control is out of their hands. If the work is so easy that they don't need to study, they are not learning much of anything about either content or control.
2. "I asked for an explanation, and then I could put the toy together myself." By getting more information, I can do things."
3. "When I look and act certain ways, people treat me differently. I can control how people react to me by what I do," If they don't practice seeing other people's point of view, children don't see their behavior as the cause of other people's reactions to them.

Involve your child in each Yearly Educational Checkup, discussing the pros and cons. What will happen if it is this way? What might happen if another way is taken? Discuss the results from last year.

Ask questions like: What effect do you think not turning in your homework had on your grade? Do you think studying for the test might have made a difference? If you really dislike that subject so much, should we explore other career choices? Can you think of anything you could try to make things work out better?

Asking questions is designed to help *your child* figure things out. The result is much different than the one you get from giving a lecture listing all the things you feel are wrong and telling how to change them. Be cautious with imposing your judgment, although you might ask your child to consider and discuss it with you.

If the plans you make together and honest efforts to implement them are not successful, find out why. Telling a child to "try harder" rarely works. Usually some adult has to help—with reading skills, appropriate reading materials, social skills, learning problems, or with some hurdle that is too high for the child to jump. If left too high, these hurdles can result in feelings of frustration and inadequacy, so the child gives up.

Hurdles need to be high enough to make jumping them a worthwhile accomplishment, but low enough for the child to clear them. When your child learns how to apply necessary skills to get over life's hurdles frequently, a sense of self control develops.

Know Yourself

Pay attention to your child's emerging potential; nourish and encourage it. Your task is to recognize your child's predispositions and capacities and then provide the richest environment you can that encourages personal development. As often as possible, allow your child to make choices from that rich environment.

Dependence, Independence and Interdependence

All children start out dependent and they stay dependent longer than most other creatures. Much of what is meant by "childhood" is the time of dependence and growth toward independence or self control. Without a sense of self control, there is no maturity, no independence. It requires the development of a self-guidance system that a person uses to function independently in society.

After achieving independence, there is a third phase of this kind of growth called interdependence; when independent people support each other and live together harmoniously and in cooperation. People who feel independent have the self-confidence to give and take with others.

Motivation:
Do You Know What Moves Your Child to Action?

Motivation is an inducement or reason to act. To be successful at schoolwork, or anything else, people need reasons to do it.

Pleasure is a reason which induces action easily. We are all ready to do what is fun or satisfying. But sometimes the longer range goal that will provide a great deal of pleasure—such as enjoyment that comes from reading or living in a pleasant home—is achieved through steps that cannot always be fun—such as learning the sounds of letters or washing dishes. With maturity, people develop the ability to see and choose what is good for them in the long run, but children sometimes have to be stimulated or impelled to do those things. (See pages 20 and 21 on Values for a related discussion.)

Intrinsic Motivation

The most valuable is intrinsic motivation. It is a fire of intensity burning within a person. Needs, desire, interests, and love that come from within trigger far more learning and achievement than any teacher would think of assigning. Intrinsic motivation impels infants to walk, talk and explore their world. When it is nourished, it incites adults to build, explore, invent, and create.

Look for the things and activities that capture and hold your child's interest. Fan that fire; encourage it to burn as brightly as it can. When one interest dies down and others increase, allow it, accept it; nurture the process. A parent's job is to value, protect and encourage such inner-directed exploration of the world.

Our natures are attracted to some things more than others. Children sometimes explore a great many areas; other children focus more narrowly. Life seems richest and more satisfying to those people who love what they do, and even children call work "play" when the inducement to do it comes from within themselves.

It is up to you to find, nurture, and guard the things that are intrinsic motivators for your child. It is possible to hinge all learning skills—such as reading, writing and arithmetic—onto an intrinsic motivator and watch it take off and develop beyond the wildest expectations of the schools.

Extrinsic Motivation

Extrinsic, or outside, motivation is better than no motivation at all. Use it if your child appears to be stalled, but bear in mind that extrinsic motivation may drive out intrinsic motivation, so be *careful*.

Continue motivating your child as you did with walking and talking—and ask the school to work with you to:

1. Encourage. Expect your child to be able, competent, responsible.
2. Reward effort and improvement with your enthusiasm.
3. Comfort and support when there are set-backs, fear, discouragement.
4. Appreciate small steps.
5. Allow and expect many trials and don't keep track of them.
6. Record only successes. Applaud them.
7. Pay attention. Actively listen, especially to feelings.
8. Provide opportunities for your child to use developing skills.
9. Be sure your child is aware of and values his or her successes.
10. Set aside lots of time for practice. Don't rush new skills.
11. Maintain limits. *You* know what is safe and what is harmful.
12. Enjoy your child. Be more of a guide and enabler, than boss or judge. Your support, love and example are valuable motivators to your child.

Discipline

It may seem strange to many parents to find the topic of discipline in a section about motivation. There are two major approaches to discipline, and many teachers and parents are worrying about only one of them, obedience. They want children to obey them, and usually they use the extrinsic motivator of punishment to accomplish the task.

There are times for obedience, of course. Parents do not want to take chances with potential disasters: their children running into the street or playing with fire, for example. If obedience is your goal, there are a few rules to follow:

1. Absolutely mean what you say. Don't make idle or extreme threats. If you are not committed to devoting the time and energy necessary to see that your child does what you say, do not say it.
2. Follow through. If homework is supposed to be done after school and it has not been, see that it is done *now. Right now.*
3. Have as few absolute rules as possible and be sure your child understands them clearly. You can discuss them, but they are not negotiable. It is never OK to run into the street without looking. *Never.*
4. Be sure your child understands the consequences of disobeying and be consistent in applying them.

You have to be careful about consequences or they can backfire. Sometimes the consequences designed to solve a discipline problem can be very harsh and defeat your overall goals of building self-esteem, a sense of inner control and interest in learning.

The second major approach to discipline is more useful for people whose goals are self-control and interdependence. It is a process of learning how to behave in ways that allow the person to fulfill his or her needs without infringing on the needs and rights of others. Although extrinsic motivators sometimes seem necessary, you tie into intrinsic motivators, showing how basic needs can be met through appropriate behavior.

Reward desired behavior. Your praise, approval, and love are basic needs for your child. Accentuate, point out, and reward things your child does that you like. You do not have a behavior problem when your child is doing things that are acceptable to you and the teachers. Provide acceptable activities for your child, activities that teach desired social skills and behavior, that encourage curiosity and growth.

Realize that you, your behavior, and your reward system are the whole world to your young child. You shape expectations and limitations early. Set up as many acceptable choices as you can. Build on positives.

Motivation and positive discipline require that you open the doors to many yeses even while teaching important noes. Self-discipline that leads to responsibility and sometimes to greatness goes far beyond obedience and punishment. You want more than a puppet. Teach cause and effect, validate your child's nature, and stay in touch with intrinsic motivation to develop genuine and lifelong self-discipline.

Values: Does Your Child Have Stars to Steer By?

Moral Development

We want our children to know right from wrong and to feel empathy for others. We want them to feel emotions, but not have to act on all of them. We want them to learn that society could not function without rules. If you have watched your children, you may have noticed how they first view rules as being very rigid. Things are either right or wrong. As they grow and encounter new experiences, children see that rules can be broken and that rules may apply to some people and not to others. So as your child grows, you will see differences in his moral reasoning about rules and behavior.

Stages of Moral Development

Lawrence Kohlberg studied the stages of moral development. At the first level, children believe that others make rules. They follow rules to avoid punishment or to gain privileges and rewards. As a parent, your rules should be reasonable and clearly understood. You must consistently enforce these rules. Inconsistency teaches children that rewards and punishment are not predictable. They may also feel that their behavior has no effect on whether they are praised or punished.

In the second level, children understand that rules are needed when playing and working with others. They understand that the classroom needs rules and that these cannot be broken. Children love rules and will make up games with many of them. Your children will want everyone to follow the rules, with no exceptions.

At the third level, children begin to question right and wrong. Discuss situations with your children and discuss moral attitudes and behaviors that may not be seen in today's society. Children may enter this level in their early teens. They begin to have personal principles and respect the rights of individuals. At the highest level, young adults base their behaviors on social order and the belief in the rights of equality and justice.

Model Appropriate Behavior

As your children grow, they go from total reliance on your values and rules to developing their own system of rules and beliefs. You can help your children develop by talking about your own values and how you developed them. Try to live so that your children can see your beliefs and values in your actions and behaviors. Talk about situations and behaviors that your children question.

Parenting Styles

You are your children's first teacher and have the greatest influence over them. You may have a preferred way of parenting. Researcher Diana Baumrind has identified three types of styles. Authoritarian parents demand obedience and expect children to not question them. Many times this style of parenting is harsh. These parents are not openly affectionate with their children, but love them very much. So there is little warmth but high control. Authoritative parents try to guide their children in the correct behaviors. They help their children think through their actions. These parents are seen as warm but demanding. Parents have their standards and expect their children to behave, but also recognize each child's strengths. Permissive parenting styles are very inconsistent. There are no set rules or guidelines; parents do not expect mature behavior. Most effective parents use the authoritative style. These children are independent, friendly, cooperative, and work hard in school. These parents explain the reasons behind their rules, and give children responsibility. They explain their expectations and tell their children they know they will meet them.

Things You Can Do To Be An Authoritative Parent

1. Help your children identify why they are behaving in certain ways. Is it out of fear, for a reward, the desire for approval from you, friends, or the teacher?
2. Discuss situations where your child or others, have demonstrated high moral behavior.
3. Children can regress to lower levels when stressed. Recognize this and discuss it with your children.
4. Talk about values and beliefs together.

Part II
The First Five Years

The most important part of your child's life is the time before school starts. You are the most important teacher your child will ever have. What you do during these years will affect everything that comes later.

Learning builds upon past learning. If your child has experienced the joy of learning, school will be a better experience than it will be for the child whose learning attempts have not been encouraged.

The Value of Play

Much of a child's learning comes through play. Play is voluntary, unthreatening, and fun. Professional baseball is not play. A group of friends going to the park for a game is usually play.

Play is the way we can explore life without fear or failure. If it is play, a person can stop at any time. If it is play, you should be able to recognize some sign of it such as laughter or smiles. Play is a valuable activity through which we learn 1) how to get along with other people; 2) about ourselves—what we like and do well; 3) new physical skills; 4) about the world—objects, places, activities; and 5) how to think and how to learn.

The more experiences children have, the more they learn. And the more they learn, the more they can learn. So put your breakable valuables out of reach and open the world to your child. Simple toys are often the most fun. Pots and pans pulled out of a cupboard intrigue children and using their imaginations they turn a cardboard box into a spaceship, a castle, or a fort.

Things that involve children actively help them to learn. Consider providing experiences with blocks, beads, balls, paint, puppets, musical instruments, and pictures in addition to natural materials such as clay, seashells, plants, and animals to help your child explore the world around him or her. Take your child into the world beyond home. Going to the store, the post office, the bank, are all opportunities for your child to learn about the world around him or her. Talk to your child about all of these experiences and attach words to them. By doing this, you are supporting the language development of your child.

Don't work at your child's education; play at it. Have fun. Enjoy it together. Follow your child's curiosity. Stop to smell the flowers. Really look at the spider and its web. Go through the wonder of a tadpole becoming a frog.

In the first six or seven months your baby needs to learn the following:

- What it is liked to be loved
- How to reach for a nearby object

In the first two years your baby needs to:

- Develop security
- Develop trust
- Feel capable and able
- Be talked to

At about age 3 or 4 your child begins to develop autonomy, which is a sense of self-control. They will be able to do things without help or outside direction. Allow your child to do as much "by myself" as possible. You can encourage autonomy and avoid developing a sense of self-doubt in your child by being patient and avoiding criticism for accidents like wetting, soiling, or breaking things.

Preschool Development

Language and math ability start developing early. You can assist with developmental tasks by spending time on them. A list of things to do to improve language and math skills before school starts appears below.

Language

- Talk with your child
- Read to your child frequently
- Encourage expression through talk, painting, dancing, singing, etc.
- Do things with your child, talking about it together while you do them
- Explain and clarify things
- Respond to your child's questions
- Encourage your child to discuss feelings with you
- Ask your child's opinion about things and listen
- Play Simon Says games to teach place words like over, under, through, and beneath and to follow directions
- Point out words that appear on household items and on street signs, etc.
- Make up rhymes
- Sing songs

Teach listening. It is as important to language development as are reading skills. The key to listening is to be sure that the listener hears what the speaker says and understands what he means. The first step is to listen to your child. Then ask, "Is this what you said?" If not, try again. Encourage your child to practice the same procedure.

The following skills should be developing before kindergarten.

- Hears differences in sounds
- Knows that letters have sounds
- Knows the sounds of some common letters
- Knows the names of letters
- Speaks in sentences
- Retells events in sequence (first, then)
- Can explain what is happening in a picture
- Knows that reading goes from left to right
- Can print and read name

Mathematics

Before your child goes to school, have fun with skills and words that are part of math and logical thinking. In fun ways, help your child begin learning the following skills:

- Knows the names of numbers
- Can count from 1 to 10
- Knows place relationships (up, down, inside, outside, on, over, under, first, next, last, before, after, between, right, left, etc.)
- Can use words for colors and sizes
- Can sort things by size (largest, next largest, smallest).
- Can sort things by color ("Put all the red beads in one pile", etc.).
- Sees likenesses and differences ("How are dogs alike? How are cats different from dogs?", etc.).
- Knows shapes and their names (circle, square, triangle)
- Can sort things by shape (all things that are round, square, etc.)
- Can draw circles, squares, and triangles
- Can discover, create, and continue patterns (string beads, point out patterns in rugs, create patterns with different shapes, etc.)
- Is able to recall and perform instructions for doing three things in a row.

Physical Developmental Record

Good physical health affects all other areas of life, including intelligence and school success. A record of early health may be especially useful if your child develops a problem in later years that a doctor or therapist will want to trace to its beginnings. You will also be asked for a birth certificate and proof of vaccinations each time you move to a new school district, so keep them with the Educational Records page.

If problems develop in school, first check the possibility of poor vision, hearing loss or childhood illnesses.

Pre-natal History

Q Full Term Q Pre-term	RH Test Q Negative Q Positive		
Problems:			

Delivery

Date:		Time:	
Place *(home or name of hospital):*	City:		State:
Doctor:			
Method *(natural, anesthetics, forceps):*			
Complications *(breech, jaundices):*			

Medical Record—*Immunizations (date of each dose):*

Diphtheria, Tetanus and Whooping Cough	1)	2)	3)	4)
Polio	1)	2)	3)	
Measles		Mumps		
Rubella		Smallpox		
TB Test Type		Date	Results	

Diseases, Illnesses — **Dates**

Diseases, Illnesses	Dates
High Fevers *(to what degree)*	
Fainting spells, convulsions	
Accidents, serious bumps on the head	
Physical handicaps	
Allergies	
Surgery *(for what)*	
Vision check results	

Hearing check results	
Dental check results	

If there is insufficient space here to record all of them, make an additional list to keep with the doctor's records of immunization.

Special Services

Some children who are intelligent and able in many ways suffer from learning disabilities that make it difficult or impossible for them to read, work with numbers, or remember even ordinary things like where they put something. Large numbers of children—over 20%—have physical, learning, or behavioral characteristics that interfere with their being able to do well in the ordinary classroom or without classroom support.

These children are sometimes called lazy and told to "try harder". Eventually they may be labeled "under achieving" or "dumb". By the end of the primary grades they are often unhappy and emotionally troubled. They may develop a fear of school, some children fake illness to escape from the feeling of failure. Others exhibit acting out behavior because they would rather be the class-clown than the class dummy. These are all symptoms and signs of a child who may need additional help.

This process assumes you have already ruled out health issues such as vision, hearing, hyper-activity etc.

Coping with the Problem

Parents may need time to accept that there is a real problem or disability. It is often difficult for parent(s) to accept the fact that their child has a disability or learning problem. But most parents, if they are honest with themselves, know when their child needs help.

Signs of not accepting or denying that there is a problem are: Anger at your child, yourself, school personnel, or experts trying to help. Remember your child's learning problem does not reflect badly on you or your child. You are your child's advocate in school! You must make it a priority to accept the situation and take action. Your child's education and future depends on it.

If You Suspect Your Child has a Disability

As a parent you know your child best. You know if they developed at a normal rate and speed. You know if they are afraid or frustrated. That is why you have to be an advocate for your child. You have to be the coach of their team as well as the cheerleader. If you suspect that your child may have a disability contact your child's teacher. Ask how he/she is doing compared to other children their age. Ask if his/her behavior is different or delayed from his/her peers. Even though you know your child, sometimes it takes seeing your child with his/her age appropriate peers to see that there is a delay. Bring a list of concerns to your child's teacher and explore possible solutions. If your child is having difficulty the teacher may suggest starting a pre-referral process to ensure that your child's delays or problems are corrected through coordinated planning between the home and the school.

If the School Suspects Your Child has a Disability

Schools are legally obligated to inform you if they feel that your child is lagging behind his/her peers either academically or socially/behaviorally. Typically the first step is coordinated planning between home and school to identify and correct any problems.

The pre-referral process brings a team of people together to help solve your child's academic or behavioral problems. Each state differs in how this works but there are several aspects that are common in most plans.

Step 1
- Teachers collect information on every child in the class to see who is on grade level and who is not. If your child exhibits behavioral problems, the teacher will record classroom observations or records.

Step 2
- Teachers use the baseline data to identify which students scored below expected. If your child is below the target he/she is at risk for school difficulties. If your child's behavior differs from that of his/her peers that too can trigger intervention from the team.

Step 3
- Next, the teacher may provide daily small group instruction to students who score below the benchmark academically. This instruction should be geared toward the child's identified weakness. If the child's behavior is deemed inappropriate a behavior plan should be enacted.

Step 4
- The teacher will monitor your child's progress toward the benchmark (skill), using frequent assessments for a specified period of time. This data should be shared with you when appropriate. If the intervention is behavioral, weekly behavior reports may be sent home.

Step 5
- The team should review, revise, or discontinue small group instruction based on whether or not your child has mastered the skill. The goal of the interventions should be for a short-term fix. The intervention should not last forever. The same is true for a behavioral intervention. Once the child learns how to behave in the classroom, the behavioral intervention should be changed or stopped.

Step 6
- For students not showing evidence of learning the skill, an increase in the intensity, duration and/or frequency of instruction should occur. For example the teacher may work with your child 1-1, or another teacher may be brought in to work with your child. The teacher should maintain some sort of record that details how your child is doing. The same is true for the behavioral intervention. Another strategy should be tried.

Step 7

- If after an intensive intervention period your child is still not making adequate progress, the team (which you are part of) should ask for a comprehensive evaluation to determine if a disability is the cause of the lack of progress. This is the first step in determining if your child is eligible for special education services. However, intervention continues during this time. The teacher should still be working in a small group or one-on-one with your child or behavioral interventions should continue.

Step 8

- After the initial team meeting, all of the data previously collected, as well as, more formal tests will be completed and an IEP (Individualized Educational Plan) team (which you are a part of) will determine whether your child has a disability and meets the criteria for special education services. If the student is eligible for special education, an IEP is developed and becomes the student's new instructional program.

For further information on the IEP process and other helpful information please see:

www.ncld.org/publications-a-more/parent-advocacy-guides/idea-parent-guide

www.ncld.org/publications-a-more/parent-advocacy-guides/a-parent-guide-to-rti

When Your Child Enters a New School

Starting a new school is usually both an exciting and a frightening experience, no matter what age it happens.

Preschool or kindergarten is a large and important break with the family. Then first grade seems like "real" school, and there is often a feeling that from then on the results really count. Junior high school is more "grown up," less childlike, and students believe that more is expected. The same increased pressure comes again when the young person enters high school.

If you move to a new neighborhood, everything changes again for your child. The challenge to adapt to a new school and the need to make new friends and can be frightening. Be prepared. With your help your child can retain enthusiasm, pride, and confidence, making each move as smooth as possible.

Discuss the changes. Together, find out what the schedules, routines and classes will be. Will "best friends" be together? How are groups assigned? What choices of teachers and subjects are available? Can you visit the school with your child before the first day of school?

Encourage your child to talk about the coming situation and ways of dealing with frightening possibilities. Perhaps it would help if you both play-act, trying out the situation in advance. Offer warmth, comfort and safety. Children sometimes go back to acting younger when they are fearful or under strain. Offer support and encouragement. As soon as your child feels safe again, self-assurance will emerge and growth continue.

Retention

If your child is retained another year in the same grade, you have a special challenge to self-esteem. Beware of falling into the trap of thinking that your child is a "failure". Did you ever hear of a parent who at some predetermined point (like June 1) called for a family conference to decide if the baby should be promoted to "running" or put back into "crawling" because he was still falling down a lot? Of course not. So keep your attention on facilitating your child's development. Don't be sidetracked onto the dead end of worrying about grade level.

Retention is most frequently advised during the primary grades. More often than not, boys mature more slowly than girls. Another year is all that is needed, in most cases, for them to sail smoothly through the school years.

Retention is also becoming more frequent as schools establish skill levels that students must meet in order to be promoted. Whether that is a good or a bad thing for your child depends on how you see it and what is done to solve the problem that caused it. Going from grade to grade means nothing in itself. Unless the appropriate material is learned, promotion can in fact become increasingly frustrating to the student.

Provide Support

As long as schools continue to use grade levels, students are inclined to measure their progress in terms of being behind, ahead, or "where they belong".

Retention will not hurt your child unless it results in permanent feelings of being a failure. Be grateful for the earliest knowledge of difficulties and make correction of the problem and your child's continued growth your only concern.

Find the places in the important skill areas, especially reading, writing and arithmetic, where your child *can* succeed. Work with teachers or tutors to provide successes, practice, growth, praise, and more success. To develop academic self-esteem, you and teachers must increase the number of your child's successes and your child's expectations of success.

Kindergarten Developmental Record

In Kindergarten there are many skills your child can learn. Be sure that going to school *aids* progress in developing self-esteem, a sense of inner control, and interest in learning. Solve problems that arise before they become complicated. If your child is unhappy, find out why. Symptoms to act on include the following:

Your child:

Isn't making progress learning
Doesn't want to go to school
Is teary and unhappy after school
Is generally unpleasant to be around

Visit the classroom and watch your child in action, if possible. Discuss the problem with the teacher so that he or she understands your concern. If the classroom is peaceful and your child is busy and interested in the activity when you visit, probably the classroom is not the problem and you can look for other possible sources. But if you sense that school is not a happy place for your child, discuss possible solutions with the teacher and your child.

Things you can do:

- Make the Yearly Educational Checkup.
- Fill out the Educational Record page.
- Get acquainted with other parents and children.
- Explore the school with your child—the building, schedule, and lunch arrangements.
- Meet the people at school with your child—the teacher, principal, secretaries, teacher.
- Listen to your child and discuss daily activities.
- Attend school meetings, open house, PTA, conferences.
- Be sure you and your child understand the teacher's rules.
- Let the teacher know that you feel that you, he/she, and your child make a team.
- Work together to support each other's plans.

You (and the school) can help your child learn *initiative* by:
- Providing opportunities for doing things physically
- Accepting fantasy and play
- Listening to and answering questions

If your child is given a kindergarten "screening" or "ability" test(s), record the following:

Tests and date	
Results	
Action Taken	

Keeping track of interests tells you something about your child's preferred ways of learning, so list the following as part of the Yearly Educational Checkup:

Favorite stories	
Favorite books	
Favorite activities	
Favorite school activities	
School friends	

Does your child need help in any area?	
Who is going to do *what, when,* to help?	

Year's goals:

Child's	
Teacher's	
Parents'	

Reading and arithmetic skills: (Check when accomplished.)

- ☐ Knows names of letters of the alphabet
- ☐ Increasing vocabulary: names things and activities
- ☐ Pays attention (doesn't interrupt)
- ☐ Recalls three items in sequence
- ☐ Recalls a three-part design
- ☐ Repeats four numbers

Again, add to these lists based on the curriculum for each grade level at your school.

This may sound premature, but now is the time to start planning for your child's college education. Many states offer pre-paid college plans that hold the price of college at today's rate.

Part III:
Grade School Ages 6 Through 12

Children reach a decision about their ability in school by the end of the primary grades based on the progress they are making and the feedback they get from teachers, parents, and peers. Their future depends largely on whether they decide that they are intelligent enough to be able to succeed. Work with the school to be sure your child's environment provides many successful learning opportunities.

Creating a Team-How to Work with the School

Considering how often your child will move from teacher to teacher and school to school, it is most helpful and more logical for you to keep track of your child's learning and to assume the responsibility of working with the teachers and your child in a three-way partnership. Meet the teachers who have your child in class. Get to know them. Join the parents' group and go to meetings. Participate! Get the information and skills you need to do your part. If the parents in your school cannot provide the information you need, perhaps the parent group would be interested in developing workshops where you can all learn. Parent groups can develop sessions in areas such as understanding test scores and cumulative records, having effective parent-teacher conferences, helping students learn at home, and encouraging interest in reading and writing.

Your role in this partnership is to help your child to:

1. *Feel good about school and develop self-confidence.* Be sure to attend school functions with enthusiasm. Listen with interest to your child's descriptions of what happened at school. Praise accomplishments. Take the time to get to know your child's friends and teachers.
2. *Go to school rested, well nourished, and happy.*
3. *Understand school rules, the reasons for them, and ways of adapting to them.*
4. *Have homework done or be prepared with questions to ask the teacher.*
5. *Plan ahead.* You can help by finding out important dates in advance (e.g. test dates and report card deadlines) and by helping your child make plans to be ready for them. Try to avoid having family activities interfere with those plans.

The Skills of Teamwork

Collaboration can be incorporated into schools if educators, parents, and students work together as a group. The goal for the group is to produce a better learning experience for the student than could be produced alone. Your PTA may want to bring in people who can help the group learn problem solving, group decision making, goals clarification, conflict resolution, and other techniques that help the group function.

Yearly Educational Checkup Steps in School Years

During school years the Yearly Educational Checkup requires bringing everyone (you, your child, and the teachers) together to determine what things need to be worked on and a plan for doing it. In short, you want to develop a yearly educational plan for your child.

The beginning of a school year is a good time for the checkup. Or, you may prefer to do it in two steps: the first in the spring, when choices are being made for the upcoming year's classes and teachers, and the second in the fall to revisit plans made earlier and to agree on goals with the newly involved teacher(s). This kind of measuring and checking in order to make plans is called formative assessment. The more of it that is done, the more the learning assignments are apt to fit your child's learning needs. Usually the time spent helping your child match the learning to his or her learning needs is pleasant, productive, quality time. Continue the steps you began earlier. You should:

1. Go through the year's Developmental Record page. Read it and discuss developmental tasks. Talk about things as you record them.

2. If your child is working at basic reading and math skills, check those skills using the appropriate pages in this handbook. Discuss how you and your child feel about progress made and next steps needed.

3. In upper elementary or from early secondary school years, go over the *Experiences* section. Work out volunteer experiences and add them to your plans. What other experiences would be good to provide this year? Add them.

4. Refer to the appropriate grade level Educational Record. Fill in all that you can. Complete it at the conference.

5. Talk about overall goals and the plans you are making. Spend most of your time listening, not telling. Discuss the pros and cons of a choice together, or encourage your child to think out loud while you listen. Ask questions that will lead your child to weigh the responsibilities connected with each possible choice. Also, ask questions to be sure you understand what your child really means. Talk about long-range goals. As your child reaches higher grades, think about high school, job goals, and advanced training or college. Talk about the kinds of classes and skills that could be developed now to help reach those goals. Make an agenda of the things you want to cover with the teacher when you go for a conference.

The School Conference

Now you are ready to take active roles in planning with the school. It probably will not be possible to complete all the following suggestions since school personnel may be limited in the amount of time they can give every family. Be prepared and accomplish as much as you can in the time you have together.

1. Call the school and ask for an appointment with the counselor, or administrator to examine your child's records. Take this book with you. Record what tests have been given and what the scores mean. How does the school use those scores? Are students grouped according to their scores? What does that mean in terms of what is taught and how? Read everything new in the record since your last visit. You have the right and responsibility to ask about entries that you think are inaccurate. You may ask for a copy of the records to keep as part of your records. Add to your agenda anything you want to discuss with the teacher**(s)** as a result of this visit.

2. Next, make an appointment with the teacher(s) for a conference. Again, take this book and your agenda with you and fill in information that applies. You may need additional time if your child is experiencing difficulties. Try not to take other children with you, but if you must take them, provide something for them to do quietly by themselves.

3. At the conference you should be able to find out what skills your child is learning in each subject. Ask the teacher to check the reading and math skills and determine the current independent reading level, which you will record on the Developmental Record page. Have your child demonstrate those skills successfully before you check them off and make plans to work on the next ones. What reading level materials does the teacher provide for learning academic subjects?

4. Record strengths as well as areas for improvement. Does your child need help? If so, develop a "who does what, when" plan and record it in this book. See samples of work done in school or take papers with you and ask, "What makes this an A or a C or a D paper?" What specific things is your child doing well or poorly? Are there practice games or activities that you can use at home to help your child learn what is being taught? Go over all the items in your agenda.

5. Be sure that you and your child understand what the teacher's goals are. Try to leave with a written copy of a specific plan. Check progress on that plan through the year by notes, phone calls, emails, or additional conferences. If your child has educational, social, or personal problems at school, you may want more frequent meetings to see how plans are working out and to make new ones.

6. Complete a checkup at home. Fill in all remaining entries on the Developmental Record page. How does your child feel about school this year? What kind of help would he or she like from you? Check your plans and record time lines on a calendar. Refer to this information often and at least once a year do a thorough job of recognizing growth and success and identifying problem areas. The checkup helps each member of the team understand, appreciate, and make a commitment to your child's growth. And that leads to success.

For Busy Parents or Single Parents

Single parents have added worries and concerns when it comes to participating on the educational team and working with the school, but those concerns are becoming widespread for couples as well. Everyone seems to be busier these days. It may be difficult to get to school during school hours, and it is often as challenging to make time to attend evening meetings. More organization is needed for working parents to do everything necessary and to enjoy their children too.

Consider fitting the following suggestions into your schedule:

1. *Have regular communication.*
    Have regular, daily positive interactions with your child. Dinner time, shopping, and doing chores are all activities that work as long as you listen, talk, and laugh together. Make it a time when you can communicate that your child's conversation is important to you, and that you enjoy time together.

2. *Make it important.*
    Make the important things in your child's life as much a priority as are the important things in your life. Ask for school conferences after working hours and go to them. Arrange to be able to reach the teacher by phone or email. Attend the play, or game, or award dinner. You make it your business to get your child or yourself to the doctor; make the Yearly Educational Checkup your business too.

3. *Plan to have fun.*
    Figure out how to have fun with your child. Make it important that you laugh together often and that you share adventures and activities together.

4. *Share the load.*
    Help your child assume increasing responsibilities in the home so you have more time to spend doing these other things. It is good for both of you when your child contributes. Be sure to balance increased responsibilities with greater privileges.

5. *Don't nag.*
    Plan the times when you have to deal with difficulties between you and your child (don't use mornings before work and school, or as soon as you get home, or before or during meals). Don't let tensions erupt into "discipline" sessions. Wait until you are calm. Separate these times from the regular good times.

When There Are School Problems

When a student is unhappy at school . . .

Something is wrong that may call for a team meeting. Being involved in your child's school life is what your child and the school wants. To ask for a meeting you can email the child's teacher, write a note, or call the main office and set up an appointment. In high school the first contact should be made with your child's guidance counselor. Help your child formulate ideas and requests ahead of time. The focus of the meeting should be "how can we help the child succeed as a student?' It is important to let your child do as much talking as possible. Be prepared to support, clarify, and help, but only when needed. Develop an action plan. Who will do what? When, will it happen? How long will it be before we check to make sure it is working? Help your child learn self-help skills.

When the school is unhappy with the student or you are unhappy with the school . . .

Again a meeting should be set up. This may be a team meeting, which would involve the principal and your child's teacher(s), or it may be a meeting with an individual teacher or guidance counselor.

If you have been asked to go to your child's school because of a problem, don't panic. Listen carefully to your child's version of the situation. Talk things over together to be sure you both understand the problem or issue. Before the conference, develop questions and suggestions that you feel may shed light on the problem or solve it.

At school let the teacher talk first. They should start the meeting highlighting the positive traits of your child and then outline any concerns or problems. Be willing to tackle behavior and learning problems early at home, but keep your perspective. Keep in mind it should be the goal of the team to develop a success plan for your child. Identify the teacher's goals. Be sure that the problem is related to your goals before you try to change your child's behavior. You should be able to work out a solution with the teacher. Teachers want to know that the home and the school are on the same page. Remember the three most important pieces of a parent-teacher conference; 1) to gather information, 2) to develop a plan and 3) to build a partnership. In order to foster building a positive relationship use the following guidelines:

- Be on time—You only have a short time with your child's teacher. Be respectful of that time.
- Bring questions—What would you like to know about classroom, academic, or social happenings? What requests do you have for the teacher? When specifically is your child having difficulty? Is it with a particular group of children? On certain days or times?
- Surface concerns—What concerns do you have about your child's performance? Bring work samples and be prepared with examples.
- Ask for examples—If the teacher doesn't get specific, ask for examples of what your child does well and needs to work on.

- Make sure you leave the meeting with a written action plan that outlines everyone's role (you, your child and the teacher) in the plan. Make an appointment to check on your child's progress.
- Say thank you—Sincerely thank the teacher for his or her time and hard work with your child.
- Keep a written log of the meeting and any paper work given to you.

Read more at:

- **Parent Teacher Conferences: Checklist www.suite101.com/content/checklist-successful-parent-teacher-conferences-a291219#ixzz1Dg4MuJI7**

- www.scholastic.com/resources/article/8-warning-signs-that-your-child-is-under-too-much-stress/

When All Else Fails

If you find that your child continues to have behavioral or academic problems the school may begin an evaluation process. If your school does not recognize problems that you see at home and you believe these problems are hurting his/her academic success, you can request a formal evaluation. This is your right under the Individuals with Disabilities Act. However, it is often a good idea to try several intervention strategies prior to requesting formal testing.

Aptitudes and Abilities

It is important to discover and encourage your child's aptitudes and abilities. All infants start out eager to become all they can become, propelled from within by a built-in need to develop themselves. Many influences in our society tend to restrict and repress that development. Your job and the school's job are to help your child fulfill his/her potential.

Intelligence

Intelligence is more process than product. Schools often measure it by means of tests, which provide a number score (intelligence quotient-IQ). No single number is an adequate measure of intelligence. Psychologists do not even agree on a definition of intelligence; much less know how to adequately measure intelligence. An IQ score may give some indication of how much your child has learned compared with other children of the same age.

IQ scores may vary from year to year. If scores come from group written tests, the chief function may be to inform schools of how well your child reads or even takes tests. It is essential that you keep track of your child's test results as part of the Yearly Educational Checkup. Be sure that teachers teach your child how to take tests (test-taking strategies, special vocabulary, what the directions mean, how to use time wisely, and so on). Multiple indicators (grades, group and individual tests, teacher assessment, parent assessment, health evaluations, private professional evaluations) over an extended period of time is the safest way to assess a child's ability.

If test scores dip downward, look for causes both at home and school. These causes may include health, the classroom environment, or forces working within your child related to the test itself: interest, motivation, self-esteem, and when or how the test is administered can all affect test scores. If you do not find the cause of the dip in scores, look into your child's learning experiences or lack of them. The experiences, both at home or school, may not be appropriate.

Left Brain, Right Brain

The human brain is divided into two parts (hemispheres). Much has been written and studied about the effects the two hemispheres—left brain, right brain—have on learning, emotions, and actions of an individual. In other words, a left-brain orientation means that an individual is controlled by the left hemisphere of the brain (left-brain dominant) and a right-brain orientation means that an individual is controlled by the right hemisphere of the brain (right-brain dominant). Everyone has both left-brain (verbal, analytic, systematic, sequential, numerical, and logical) and right brain (spatial, random, intuitive, global and creativity) abilities.

Most schools tend to be left-brain oriented emphasizing skills involved in talking, reading, writing, mathematics, evaluating, and solving problems through data rather than right-brain oriented which involves activities that include seeing several solutions to a problem, solving problems starting with the whole picture, seeing patterns, understanding relationships, synthesizing, and dealing with space and movement. As a result, children who are left-brain dominant may be more successful in school than those who are right-brain dominant.

The internet can provide inventories to determine if your child is right or left brain oriented or you can check with your physician.

Learning Plateaus

The brain grows in spurts up to the age of 16, with periods in between when children may seem to be less able or interested to learn. Since girls often mature faster than boys and gifted children faster than others, these periods may differ. Intelligence may be like this, as well. Be willing to ride the tide of your child's growth and development towards brave new accomplishments and enjoy the quieter time of practicing and integrating those skills.

Record of Aptitudes and Abilities

Grade	What makes your child happiest? Activity	Age	Awards, Honors, Achievements
1			
2			
3			
4			
5			
6			
7			
8			
9			
10			
11			
12			

Age	Talents, Things Done Well	Age	Awards, Honors, Achievements

Mental Ability or Scholastic Aptitude Tests

Date	Results	Date	Results

Helping Your Child Learn to Read and Write

Parents play an important role in how well their children learn to read and write. It is not enough that children learn the skills of reading and writing. They must enjoy these activities. A key to school success is an interest in reading and writing. Children may need help in seeing why reading is important.

Children develop language very early. Children show they are ready to read when they become interested in sounds and rhymes and realize that the print on the pages has meaning. There is much you can do to help your child in these areas.

Good Beginnings

1. Read to your children. This is the most important thing you can do for your children before they begin school. You can continue this until your children express a desire to read alone. Select stories, myths, fantasy, history, science or sports and see which type your child prefers.
2. Spend time having fun with books, words, sounds and writing.
3. Praise each small success just as you did when your children learned to walk and talk.
4. Talk about the sounds of letters and what words mean. Have real conversations about everything. Listen carefully when they speak, respond to questions, ask questions, and discuss things.
5. Turn off the television and computer for a definite period of time each evening. Spend the time talking, telling stories, reading or looking at books or playing word games.
6. If finances permit, purchase an electronic "tablet" for your child. With proper supervision and controls these devices can open up significant learning opportunities. Some school districts are purchasing electronic reading devices in lieu of textbooks.
7. Write what your child says and then have him or her "read" it to you. Draw pictures to go with the writing and make a book out of it to "read" later.
8. Have your children write notes, take phone messages, make shopping or "to do" lists.
9. Have books, newspapers and magazines in your home. Spend time together when everyone reads. Give books for gifts. Take your children to the library and let them choose books to read at home.
10. Have your children read to do something, following a recipe or directions for building a model or playhouse.

11. Build their knowledge about words. Connect words to action, places, things and directions. Read road signs, menus, and cereal packages. Vocabulary is a major part of reading and writing. Children begin school with a speaking vocabulary between 2,400-17,000 words. Children with larger vocabularies find school easier.

School Reading Program

Your child's reading program should include five essential components: phonemic awareness, phonics, fluency, vocabulary, and reading comprehension.

1. Phonemic awareness is knowing that words are made up of individual sounds. Your child should be able to rhyme, pick out syllables in spoken words, tell the first and last sounds in a word, and separate the sounds in a word. Teaching sounds along with the letters of the alphabet is important for later reading and writing.

2. Phonics is the relationship between sounds and letters. Children must know that letters represent sounds. Phonics instruction is most effective when it starts in kindergarten or first grade. Older students need ongoing instruction, but also instruction in spelling, fluency and comprehension. If your child is in kindergarten, first or second grade, make sure that phonics instruction is included as a part of reading. If your child is older and having difficulty reading, find out if phonics would benefit his program.

3. Fluency is the ability to read accurately and quickly. Readers do not have to concentrate on the sounds of words, but can focus on the meaning of the text. This is the step between recognizing words and comprehension. Practice helps children become automatic, rapid readers. Provide home opportunities for your child to practice reading.

4. Vocabulary is knowing what words mean. There are four vocabularies: listening, speaking, reading and writing. Words in these vocabularies may be different although some words will overlap. Children beginning to read use oral vocabularies to recognize the words in a book. It is much easier for them to read words that are familiar to them. Children learn vocabulary directly and indirectly. Direct methods include teaching individual words and their meanings, dictionary usage, and using word parts to figure out meaning. Indirect methods include conversations, listening to adults read to them, and personal reading. Your child's program should include both direct and indirection teaching.

5. Reading comprehension is understanding and remembering what has been read. At each grade level, your child should be taught strategies for getting meaning from the text. These strategies include your child knowing when he understands what he is reading.

Reading and Writing Problems

If your child is having a reading or writing problem, do not panic, pressure or push your child. Here are some areas you need to explore:

1. How well does your child read? Ask your child's teacher to suggest reading materials on the appropriate level. Read short selections each night and then ask who, what, when, where and why questions about the passage.
2. Ask your teacher for a list of reading skills that need attention.
3. How much time does the school spend on skills and what methods are used for teaching. Ask the teacher to send home information on what you can do to support schoolwork.
4. Poor reading/writing skills can have a negative impact on all subjects. If your child sees more than one teacher for academic subjects make sure they provide input.
5. If your child has difficulty in a subject area, are there reading materials available on his reading level?

Once you know your child's strengths and areas of concern, you and the school can work together to find the appropriate materials. You can provide the encouragement and lots of practice. There are games (with directions that need to be read), songs, riddles, drama and other opportunities for enjoyable reading activities. A word of warning: If you find that you are doing more coaxing, forcing or yelling than teaching, stop! This is not enjoyable for either of you. It is better to find an older student or tutor who likes to work with children and who would enjoy teaching reading. A positive support attitude is the most important element that you can provide at home.

Reading Skill Record

The information in the first column of the Reading Skill Record should be verified for your school since this can vary from one school district to another. Change the grade levels where necessary. Record the month and year that lessons begin for each of the skills in the second column. You can get this information from the teacher. Check off the skills in the third column when no further attention is needed.

Notice that most of the basic skills are taught before the fourth grade. If your child has not learned them, *do no panic*, but **do** make it your business to see that help is provided, by the teacher, by you, or by a tutor. *Your child should not be receiving instruction in higher level skills until those taught first are learned.* Provide a great deal of reading material at the Independent reading level for practice of skills being learned.

	Grade Level	Started	Learned
Associates consonant sounds with letters: b, c, d, f, g, h, j, k, l, m, n, p, r, s, t, v, w, y, z	1		
Knows sounds of 2 letter blends: sl, pl, cl, bl, fl, gl, st, sc, sk, sm, sn, cr, pr, fr, br, gr, tr, dr, nt, nd, sw, tw	1		
Knows sounds when 2 letters make one sound: sh, ch, th, wh, ph, ng, gh, ck, kn, wr, gn	1		
Knows that a, e, I, o, u can have more than one sound (long/short)	1		
Developing vocabulary, recognizes some words in print	1		
Can tell the main idea of a story	1		
Can give details of story read silently	1		
Reads for pleasure	1		
Knows consonant sounds	2		
Knows 2 letter consonant blends (see listed with grade 1)	2		
Knows 3 letter beginning blends: spl, spr, str, thr	2		
Knows short vowel sounds (at, bit, us)	2		
Knows long vowel sounds (ate, bite, use)	2		
Understands y can be a vowel like i (fly) or a consonant (as in yes)	2		
Uses possessives ('s, s', es')	2		
Uses contractions (they'll, isn't)	2		
Understands root words (fun ny)	2		
Can alphabetize with first letter	2		
Predicts what will happen next in a story	2		
Finds proof for ideas	2		
Uses table of contents in a book	2		
Reads more rapidly silently than out loud	2		
Reads 220 common sight words (get list from teacher)	3		
Reads and uses forms of address-Miss, Mrs., Mr., Ms.	3		
Knows 2 sounds of c-cat, cut, comb; city, cent	3		
Knows 2 sounds of g-germ, gin; give, gave, got	3		
Forms plurals-girls, wishes, men, lives	3		
Knows that x sounds like "cks" (box)	3		
Divides words into syllables (rab/bit) between two consonants	3		
Divides words into syllables after a vowel, before a consonant (wa/ter)			
Draws logical conclusions	3		
Sees relationships	3		

	Grade Level	Started	Learned
Uses a book's index	3		
Can read a map or chart	3		
Follows directions read out loud by another	3		
Learns many new words in content fields (science, math)	4		
Uses new words	4		
Knows what prefixes and suffixes are (*un*happ*iest*)	4		
Can use a dictionary	4		
Can pick best meaning in dictionary for use of a word in a story	4		
Can identify a topic sentence in a paragraph	4		
Can summarize reading	4		
Selects important facts to remember	4		
Uses study guides and outlines	4		
Arranges ideas in sequence	4		
Can tell story in own words	4		
Can explain relationships of characters (brothers, boss)	4		
Can tell author's mood	4		
Can give the author's purpose	4		
Can outline-knows form	4		
Learns many new words in content areas	5		
Gets meaning of unknown words from sense of the story	5		
Uses magazines and newspapers	5		
Uses reading for different purposes: pleasure; hobbies; life plans; work plans; needs	5		
Has a favorite author	5		
Knows more than one meaning of words	6		
Takes notes well	6		
Knows how to skim, survey	6		
Can use a library computer to find books	6		
Knows how libraries are organized	6		
Reads different material at different speeds	6		
Can read 180 wpm in fiction at grade level, silently	6		
Learning many new words in content areas	7-9		
Interprets what the author means	7-9		
Recognizes different reading skills needed in different content subjects	7-9		

	Grade Level	Started	Learned
Increases vocabulary through wide reading	H.S.		
Has and keeps a regular study schedule	H.S.		
Uses a thesaurus	H.S.		
Applies problem-solving approach	H.S.		
Gets information from many sources	H.S.		
Develops ideas from many sources	H.S.		
Forms own ideas about authors' qualifications	H. S.		
Judges whether statements are true	H. S.		

Helping Your Child Learn Mathematics

Success in mathematics has two parts. One is knowing number skills, facts, and processes. The second is developing a logical, problem-solving way of thinking. Both are valuable and important in math education. Even in times when calculators and computers are readily available, it is still necessary to know how to turn questions into math problems.

Attitude Is Crucial

Most children are able to learn math. Many children can also learn to enjoy math. The popular myths that few children have "math aptitude" or that girls are not good at math have been proven wrong. Children who begin school with a good vocabulary, math skills, and an attitude that numbers are fun have an early advantage. Parents can keep learning alive by continued interest and support of school work and finding opportunities to have fun practicing new skills at home.

It has been shown that the amount of time learners spend on the learning task makes the most difference in how well they learn it. It is important for your child to be able to master some skills before moving on since many math skills build on previous ones. Also, ask for related games and activities that you can use at home to support the learning. When working with your child, be patient and be playful. Keep using numbers and get your child to use them whenever possible.

Keep Track of Skills

By the end of fifth grade, most math processes have been taught. These include addition, subtraction, multiplication, and division of whole numbers (1, 2, 3), decimals (.50, .05), fractions (¼, ½), and percents (50%, 5%). Most school programs also teach problem solving, estimating, concepts of a three-dimensional world (geometry, squares, boxes, pyramids, globes, etc.), skills in measuring distance, time, weight, and temperature, and the use of tables, charts, and graphs. *Check your school and state math standards for specific math expectations.*

If your child has passed beyond a targeted grade level without acquiring one or more of the designated skills, seek help from the school. A plan needs to be made showing what everyone (teacher, parent, child, others) will do to help him/her acquire the skills in a manner that maintains a love of numbers, and builds confidence.

Mathematic Skills Record

The number in the first column tells you when the skill is usually taught in school. Record in the second column when instruction begins for each skill, asking the teacher for assistance during each Yearly Educational Checkup. In the third column, check off the skills that are well enough known that no further attention is needed. If you have questions about any of the skills, ask the teacher to go through the process with your child before you check it off.

If your child has not learned most of the essential math skills by the end of fifth grade make it your business to see that help is provided—by the teacher, by you, or by a tutor. If you use this book as recommended, you should be able to avoid crisis situations regarding your child's progress. One of the important goals of this book is for you to know how your child is doing in school **at all times.** Keep track of skills each time you do the Yearly Educational Checkup.

Arithmetic Skill Record

The information in the first column of the Arithmetic Skill Record should be verified for your school since this can vary from one school district to another. Change the grade levels where necessary. Record the month and year that lessons begin for each of the skills in the second column. You can get this information from the teacher. Check off the skills in the third column when no further attention is needed.

Notice that most essential arithmetic skills are taught by the end of the fourth grade. If your child has not learned them by the fifth grade, *do no panic*, but **do** make it your business to see that help is provided-by the teacher, by you, or by a tutor.

	Grade Level	Started	Learned
Can count from 1-100	1		
Understands the concept of tens and ones	1		
Understands and uses + or - signs correctly	1		
Adds and subtracts numbers through 10	1		
Can tell what hour and half-hour of the day it is	1		
Knows money vocabulary and value from one cent to fifty cents	1		
Identifies halves and quarters (1/2, 1/4) and knows their meaning	1		
Understands the concept of zero	1		
Knows cup, pint, quart	1		
Knows inch and half inch	1		
Can count to 999	2		
Adds three numbers, each less than 10 (2 + 4 + 5 =11)	2		
Adds and subtracts using two-digit numerals	2		
Identifies 1/3, 3/4, 2/3	2		
Knows the meaning of "fraction"	2		
Knows money value from 1¢ to $1.00	2		
Measures feet and inches	2		
Tells time to quarter hour and 5 minute intervals	2		
Knows gallons	2		
Can count numbers to 999,999	3		
Adds and subtracts with three-digit numbers	3		
Estimates sums and differences	3		
Understands multiplication and division and x and ÷ signs	3		
Knows multiplication tables through 5	3		
Can multiply using a three-digit numeral and a one-digit multiplier	3		
Can divide using a three-digit numeral and a one-digit divisor to obtain a two digit quotient	3		
Knows form for division with remainders	3		
Can convert gallons to quarts, quarts to pints, pounds to ounces	3		
Reads temperature on thermometer	3		
Knows inch, centimeter, yard, meter, foot	3		
Can read circle and bar graphs	3		
Can tell clock time	3		
Understands day, week, month	3		
Knows Roman numerals	3		
Solves basic addition and subtraction number sentence problems	4		
Adds and subtracts whole numbers using numerals to five digits	4		
Adds and subtracts fractions with different denominators	4		
Can rename fractions in higher or lower terms 2/3 = 4/6 = 8/12	4		
Adds and subtracts using mixed numerals	4		

	Grade Level	Started	Learned
Adds and subtracts money	4		
Knows multiplication tables through 10	4		
Multiplies by two-digit numbers	4		
Knows liter, kilometer, square inch, cubic inch	4		
Understands "if . . . then" logic	4		
Can read double bar and linear graphs	4		
Knows decimals to hundreds	5		
Understands place value to billons	5		
Solves word problems requiring adding, subtracting, multiplying or dividing	5		
Can add, subtract, multiply and divide fractional numbers	5		
Can divide using a two-digit divisor with a dividend of more than 3 digits	5		
Can multiply with whole and fractional numbers or mixed fractions	5		
Can add and subtract through hundredths	5		
Knows century, square foot and yard, cubic foot and yard, ton, gram	5		
Can use a ruler correctly	5		
Can find averages	5		
Understands statements using all, some or none	5		
Understand statements disagreeing with all, some or none	5		
Understands statements of "if not . . . then" logic	5		
Rounds numbers to nearest 10, 100, or 1,000	5		
Estimates answers to problems by rounding	5		
Understands negative numbers	6		
Can add and subtract with decimals to hundredths	6		
Can multiply and divide using decimal fractions	6		
Can find percent of whole numbers	6		
Understands squaring and square root	6		
Can rename a decimal in fraction form	6		
Can solve word problems involving percent	6		
Can solve word problems involving different operations	7		
Social applications of arithmetic: keeping a check book	7		
checking a bank statement	7		
figuring interest, percent costs	7-8		
budgeting	7-8		
reading maps, figuring mileage	7-8		
measure	7-8		
speed, time, distance	7-8		
Review of +,—, ÷, x operations	7-8		

First Grade Developmental Record

A good start is important for your child this year. Fill out the First Grade Education Record. You may need to ask your child's teacher for information regarding what tasks and skills should be covered this year.

The developmental task for this age is initiative, so be sure you allow your child to do things physically—at home, at school, and outdoors; accept fantasy and play and listen to and answer questions. This is the age of inquisitiveness. It is important to foster physical fitness in your child. Help your child develop a daily exercise routine. This can be done as a family or in group-play with other children.

Favorite books:
1.
2.
3.

Favorite school subjects:
1.
2.
3.

What makes him/her the happiest:
1.
2.
3.

Talent or things well done:
1.
2.
3.

Loves to do:
1.
2.
3.

Awards, honors and achievements:
1.
2.
3.

Friends:
1.
2.
3.

Strengths:
1.
2.
3.

Area(s) where help is needed:
1.
2.
3.

Who will do what and when to help:
Teacher

Parent

Student

Others

Second Grade Developmental Record

A healthy second grader feels comfortable and content as a person; is loving and lovable; needs companionship but also a time and place to be alone; feels okay about expressing feelings, even anger or fear; and is creative.

Your child may now be developing the mental ability to apply logic to specific concrete problems and understand part-whole relationships. Rules begin to make sense, as does cause and effect. Don't expect your child to solve verbal problems for a while yet, or to analyze future possibilities. Focus new mental games you play together on specific, concrete problems and you will have fun in this new developmental area.

Allow your child to make, do and build things. Provide time and opportunity for them to finish products. Offer praise, recognition and rewards for results. Keep up your child's physical fitness goals. Team sports or organized sports may be introduced at this level.

Favorite books:
1.
2.
3.

Favorite school subjects:
1.
2.
3.

What makes him/her the happiest:
1.
2.
3.

Talent or things well done:
1.
2.
3.

Loves to do:
1.
2.
3.

Awards, honors and achievements:
1.
2.
3.

Friends:
1.
2.
3.

Strengths:
1.
2.
3.

Area(s) where help is needed:
1.
2.
3.

Who will do what and when to help:
Teacher

Parent

Student

Others

Third Grade Developmental Record

Your third grader is continuing the development of reasoning and emotional stages described for second grade. Continue playing games involving deductive reasoning and figuring things out. Your child will understand rules, and may like creating his/her own rules.

It is important for your child to feel a sense of power or ability and competence within some areas. To encourage your child's development:
- Provide tasks that increase independence.
- Listen—*actively listen* by looking at your child and asking questions that shows you understand.
- Know your child's friends and their parents.
- Establish clear family "rules" and discuss them. Be sure your child knows which ones are not negotiable. Aim for consistency in all areas. Establish a clear system of rewards and consequences.

Continue to support your child's physical fitness goals. This should include healthy eating and exercise habits. They are at the age where they can make both good and bad food choices.

Favorite books:
1.
2.
3.

Favorite school subjects:
1.
2.
3.

What makes him/her the happiest:
1.
2.
3.

Talent or things well done:
1.
2.
3.

Loves to do:
1.
2.
3.

Awards, honors and achievements:
1.
2.
3.

Friends:
1.
2.
3.

Strengths:
1.
2.
3.

Area(s) where help is needed:
1.
2.
3.

Who will do what and when to help:
Teacher

Parent

Student

Others

Fourth Grade Developmental Record

Your fourth grader is likely to be on the way to feeling capable and competent. He or she can solve problems, read for answers to questions, and explore the world in many ways. You must encourage that independence and help your child develop responsibility. Although there can be many hobbies and interests at this age, your child will not excel in all of them. Promote ample opportunities for success. Encourage exploration. Provide as many opportunities for your child to interact with and learn about different parts of the world.

Continue the development of *industry* and the prevention of *inferiority*. Fill out the Fourth-Grade Educational Record. Do the Yearly Educational Checkup.

Favorite books:
1.
2.
3.

Favorite school subjects:
1.
2.
3.

What makes him/her the happiest:
1.
2.

3.

Talent or things well done:
1.
2.
3.

Loves to do:
1.
2.
3.

Awards, honors and achievements:
1.
2.
3.

Friends:
1.
2.
3.

Strengths:
1.
2.
3.

Area(s) where help is needed:
1.
2.
3.

Who will do what and when to help:
Teacher

Parent

Student

Others

Fifth Grade Developmental Record

A fifth grader spends a great deal of time with projects, books, friends, and exploring the world of things, people, and fantasy. The child is now deeply involved with friends. Know your child's friends and activities and keep open communication. Children who reach adolescence with open family communication are far more likely to stay on track during adolescence.

A daily "family time" is helpful. Turn all media off for a period of time every evening. Talk and listen to each other. Read together, play games, sing songs, learn dances, make music, share hobbies or projects, build something, explore the neighborhood. Encourage independence and exploration beyond the family. Help your child join school clubs, A Boy or Girl Scout troop, church groups, neighborhood classes in music or sports, or the YMCA. Also try to share what you know of the world, its people, cultures, and places.

Industry is still the developmental task. Encourage it and prevent *inferiority*. Do the Yearly Checkup.

Favorite books:
1.
2.
3.

Favorite school subjects:
1.
2.
3.

What makes him/her the happiest:
1.
2.
3.

Talent or things well done:
1.
2.
3.

Loves to do:
1.
2.
3.

Awards, honors and achievements:
1.
2.
3.

Friends:
1.
2.
3.

Strengths:
1.
2.
3.

Area(s) where help is needed:
1.
2.
3.

Who will do what and when to help:
Teacher

Parent

Student

Others

Sixth Grade Developmental Record

Many children attend middle school for grades 6, 7, and 8. **At** this time your child is entering a period of change and adjustment. Many children now mature physically, socially and emotionally at earlier ages. You will see increasingly wider individual differences in all of these areas among young people of your child's age for the next few years. That wide range is perfectly normal and by the time they are 18-20 years old, the differences in maturity will be less extreme. Don't worry, and don't push or hold back.

Continue nurturing and building on strengths as your child continues his or her own unique development. This may be more difficult. You may want to offer more guidance as you anticipate the challenge ahead and your child increasingly wants to do it himself. Keep in mind that no one ever learned to walk without falling down. Provide safe places to practice; offer comfort and reassurance when the falls occur; encourage brave effort and reward successes as your child stumbles, falls and eventually strides confidently to maturity.

Continue:

- Family time daily if possible (eating a meal together), but definitely frequently.
- Active listening—especially to feelings.
- Knowing and including your child's friends in family activities.
- Maintaining standards so your child knows the limits
- Supporting and encouraging physical fitness goals

Your child is probably still developing initiative and independence. Some who mature early will be entering the *role identity stage.*

Favorite books:
1. _____
2. _____
3. _____

Favorite school subjects:
1. _____
2. _____
3. _____

What makes him/her the happiest:
1. _____
2. _____
3. _____

Talent or things well done:
1. _____
2. _____
3. _____

Loves to do:
1. _____
2. _____
3. _____

Awards, honors and achievements:
1. _____
2. _____
3. _____

Friends:
1. _____
2. _____
3. _____

Strengths:
1. _____
2. _____
3. _____

Area(s) where help is needed:
1. _____
2. _____
3. _____

Who will do what and when to help:
Teacher
_____

Parent
_____

Student
_____

Others
_____

Part IV
Secondary School Ages
12 through 18

Your child is approaching adolescence, which can be challenging for all of you. The stakes are high. It is important for your child to begin to explore the adult world and find a place that fits him or her.

Physical Maturity

For many children, adolescence is extremely difficult. They must cope with puberty in physical, emotional, and social ways. The physical growth spurt can cause them to feel awkward and embarrassed. Their chemistry is volatile, often causing sudden, intense, and puzzling changes of mood. Those who mature earliest usually have the highest self-esteem. Late developers often feel inadequate and embarrassed at being still a child among their peers.

Parents need to provide constant reassurance and support. Remember Maslow's basic needs (p. 7) and that the needs of belonging, esteem by others, and self-esteem are now related to the peer group. Continue to support your child's self-esteem and self control.

Peer Group Pressures

When their child reaches adolescence, many parents awaken to the influence other young people have on their teenager as though it just emerged. That is not the case. The peer group becomes an influence in the development of children in their preschool years and continues to grow throughout the school years.

Often parents are not paying attention during the early years to their children's choice of friends or to the social behavior they are learning. Parents seem surprised and sometimes shocked when childhood friendship groups assume their more independent adolescent shapes. Parents talk to each other about "bad kids" leading their "good child" astray. That seldom happens, except when a lonely child finds it easy and appealing to move into a group he/she might not otherwise have chosen. The media talks about the generation gap and the youth culture that replaces parents as the dominating influence in lives of adolescents. The gap does not have to appear and in fact does not appear if parents have built communication channels and family foundations of mutual respect and affection.

As early as preschool years, children learn how to interact with peers toward the social maturity and independence that parents hope comes into full bloom by adolescence. Being accepted into a peer group depends on children's skills and values. It is easiest for those children who are friendly, unaggressive, and not overly dependent on their parents. Parents who help their children develop autonomy and a sense of self control based on solid values do not have a great deal to worry about during their child's adolescence.

Keep in mind that belonging is a basic need. If the need is not met, problems may occur for your child. Being a member of a peer group becomes increasingly important to children as they go through school. Children learn how to give up their personal desires to be part of a group, which is a sign of growth insofar as they learn how to cooperate with others. However, they may give up too much to be part of the group if they have no meaningful values of their own; if their self-esteem is weak; if their parents do not help them sort out conflicting demands and give them a firm emotional base of support from which to handle those demands.

Children take the strengths and weaknesses they have developed at home with them when they move into the world of peers. During the school years, they seek to create a new security system outside the home, looking for friends who share the same feelings, problems, interests, and activities.

Peer groups evolve to meet the needs of the group members, such as a desire to either escape or to commiserate with each other about adult supervision and a wish to spend time with like-minded peers who accept and understand them. The peer group becomes the haven where individuals are accepted, where they can derive pleasure and approval by being themselves, where they can learn and grow. There is not just one peer group in most children's lives. Wise parents provide choices and work with their children to help them learn how to fit into groups that meet their needs.

Schools encompass many different groups, each with its own motives, structure and requirements for membership. There will be a hierarchy of peer groups with a school that spreads from the most popular to the least popular. For example football players and cheerleaders may be the most popular group. Other groups may form around preferred clubs or school activities such as the newspaper and the yearbook staffs, the drama club or school play participants, the marching band, other athletic groups, the chess team or biology club.

Other groups form to defend themselves and their self-esteem against the assault of failure in school. They become the "tough" groups. Other adolescents join together to comfort and support each other because they feel unattractive, inept. Many adolescents go through high school with a peer group existing of one or two "best friends," All peer groups are selective, taking in new members based on age, sex, appearances, and other criteria that vary from group to group.

Popularity in school can be connected to participation in the most respected activities—athletics, academics, or demonstrating expertise in some areas other than athletics. The most popular students usually can do many things well, are cooperative and friendly, and are considered intelligent. Of course only a few people can be homecoming queen, the captain of the football team or class president. Yet these individuals set the tone. If the values and goals of the popular people are different from others' values and goals, difficult choices are inevitable and it is hard not to go to the parties or to be separate from the "popular" crowd.

When sex, fast cars, drugs, and alcohol are accepted by the dominant group, teenagers who choose not to participate in those activities must have other options that will meet their need for approval and acceptance.

Adolescents are able to resist peer pressure when they feel sure of their own beliefs, have a sense of self control, and possess high self-esteem. They rely on their friends for ordinary everyday decisions, and their friends may have a lot to do with how they talk, dress, wear their hair, and their mannerisms and recreational activities. Most adolescents, however, want to lean on their parents for important matters.

Parents need to be available and helpful without dominating and dictating. There are many ways parents can help adolescents handle peer pressure. Parents can help their children associate with others with similar values by providing them opportunities to participate with like-minded groups. Help your adolescents think through conflicting demands of any groups they are in and support them when they make the tough but good choice. You will find adolescence easiest when your child has a choice of peer groups. Most adolescents select their friends for the same social class as their parents; consequently the peer group shares many of the same values, although sometimes those values may be expressed in ways that surprise the adults. Remember that the peer group has excessive influence when the developing child does not have warm, close relationships with people of many ages. Schools usually segregate children by age groups, so you need to encourage your child's participation in activities with people of many ages. In that way your child will benefit from different points of view from valued, respected sources.

The goal is to help your teenager use the adolescent years to develop the independence and autonomy of adulthood. Peer pressure is an especially powerful current in the lives of adolescents. Your home must provide lifelines of emotional support to help your child develop a strong rudder to navigate the passage to adulthood.

Family Relationships

For real autonomy to develop, adolescents need to question and examine the standards of the family. Some parents support and guide the process; while others fight or ignore it. Teenagers rebel most strongly against authoritative, dominating parents whose discipline is generally forceful. There is no discussion of standards in these families, and the adolescent usually feels that the parents do not understand him/her. Adolescents *must* either fight or escape that control in order to develop the skills to establish a healthy adult life. When parents exert little or no control, teenagers become angry and resentful, feeling that their parents do not care what happens to them. Usually the parents are "too busy" to discuss things, and adolescents feel alone and ignored, often frightened and insecure behind a façade of self-assurance.

Family relationships that are built on respect for each person's participation and interdependence provide a support system which makes adolescence easier. There is less difficulty for young people who know themselves, can examine their values, ask questions, and explore ideas openly.

Identity, a Critical Task

The developmental task of adolescence and one of the most important things a person does in a lifetime is to *develop an identity*. Developing an *identity* is integrating and understanding all of the roles and the different pieces of the self, forming a whole that makes sense and allows for continuing self-development. Without *identity*, a person remains immature and *role confusion* results.

Developing identity is difficult, no one can do it for another person, and many people do not accomplish it. This is absolutely a do-it-yourself task. Much of what you can do as a parent, you have already established, but you can support, encourage, and help your adolescent work through the development of the most positive *identity* as possible. Your role is to listen, accept, support, clarify and point out positive things your child may not see.

Following are some questions you may use to guide the discussion with your teenager.

Questions to ask	Parent Response/Task
In what ways are you lovable?	Suggest, support
In what ways are you responsible?	Point out/praise
What things do you choose to do?	Listen, accept
What things do you choose not to do?	Discuss, accept
What is right about you?	Suggest, support
Whose approval is important to you?	Listen, accept
Whose approval is not important to you?	Accept, discuss
Are you listening to your inner voice?	Listen, accept
What does it say?	Accept, clarify

The Secondary School Years

When your child enters secondary school, find out all you can about it. Find out what the graduation requirements are, what choices of programs are available, and which ones match your teenager's personality, interests, and goals. Work with the school to help your child make good choices. Your input in promoting your teen's active participation in constructive, worthwhile activities at school and in the community can be wise insurance against trouble.

Dual Ambivalence

Keep in mind that this is the time your teenager is developing independence and there maybe differences of opinion between you. If you have maintained communication channels, you will be able to work these differences out together. Communication may be more difficult now because of the often conflicting dual ambivalence you and your adolescent will experience about your child's preparations to leave the nest. Ambivalence means being pulled in two contradictory directions. The teenager wants to go, but also has times of wanting to stay. Parents want their teenagers to mature and leave home, but they do not want to let go.

Conflict develops when one member of the family is talking from fear/protection and the other is talking from growth/adventure. When this happens, talk about these differences between you. Negotiate a solution based on respect for each other's feelings. Keep in mind that this is a transition period. Your adolescent feels and acts like a child sometimes and like an adult at other times.

If There Are Problems

If there is trouble or misunderstanding between you and your teenager, *talk about it with, not at, your teenager*. Use reasonable tones and express your concerns. Ask for your teen's point of view. Do not buy phony reasoning that goes against family values and limits, but try to see things from the point of view of an adolescent. Let your teen know you care enough to prevent his/her destruction, no matter what it takes, and you want to help and support healthy independence. Remember, we start to lay the ground work for moments like this even before they enter school.

If friends are involved, you might want to talk with the other parents. Be careful not to place blame on the other young people. People choose friends with whom they are comfortable. The "wrong crowd" cannot lead your "good child" astray all by itself. If you respect and communicate well with the teachers, counselor, or principal at school, alert them to the problem and enlist help. Give encouragement, support, and discipline toward solving the problem.

Sometimes for one reason or another, children quit school, leave home, and may get into trouble. Parents and teenagers reach the point where they agree to disagree. Don't slam the door or burn bridges. Leave the way open to get back together. Be sure your teenager knows the door is open whenever he/she wants to become part of the family again. Let your teenager know of your love even if you cannot tolerate the present behavior.

Experiences

Experience is the way to accumulate firsthand knowledge from which one's sense of competency and control develops.

Volunteer Experience

This society has few built-in roles for young people, yet all people need to feel they are useful. Teenagers especially need it because of their idealism and their search for a role in life. Help your child find ways to fill a valued place in the community and the family. Many schools have service project requirements for graduation. There is no shortage for opportunities for young people to be useful. They may need help in thinking about the idea, finding the opportunities, and making the connections. Many organizations—hospitals, senior citizen's residence homes, community parks—are just a few places that welcome volunteers.

The service performed by young people, while valuable for the people they help, also helps the young people. It often gives them their first letter of recommendation in that valuable area of experience. Volunteer references tell as much about reliability, performance, attitudes, and other important characteristics as do references from paid positions.

Career Experiences

The time to make important life choices comes earlier than many parents and children realize. Successful people explore and develop abilities, set goals, and make the most of opportunities at school. For example, the choice of high school programs begins in the eighth grade. The decision to take or not take the "hard" subjects like mathematics or chemistry is certainly not irreversible. Many young people, however, find they need more education once they get out in the world. At the same time, it is possible for young people to get into the world earlier and have experiences that will help them make better decisions along the way.

Following are some questions you can ask your adolescent that can help with educational decisions over the high school years.

- What kinds of jobs involve the things you like to do and do best? Explore them.

- Talk to people who do the jobs. Find out all you can about them.

- Would you really like that kind of work? Find out. Look for a part-time or summer job, volunteer work, or a work-study program.

- Do you have the right high school plan to prepare you for that education, or do you need to see your counselor to make changes? Is there a way you can begin getting the education now?

Setting Goals

Successful people set their own goals. They decide where they want to go and then figure out how to get there. It is the difference between drifting along with the winds and current and navigating a desired course using the rudder and sails to take advantage of the wind and current.

Help your teenager identify his/her goals. Explore the possibilities together. Set goals together frequently, and develop plans for reaching them. Yearly goals are a part of each Developmental Record. Talk with your child about past goals and how well he/she met them. Discuss how and why the goals have changed over the years.

During each Yearly Educational Checkup discuss the following with your child:
- Activities always found unpleasant
- Activities that attracted him/her.
- Where has he/she functioned as an effective part of a team?
- Where has he/she been willing to risk failure?

Identifying a Vocation

Vocation means a "calling" to do something. We each need to decide what we are called to do. It is determined by inner preferences and abilities. If we are in touch with those preferences, we can match them with an occupation.

Sometimes people do not know if they fit into an occupation until they try it. A person should feel that it is acceptable to get out of the wrong occupation and into another that is more of a vocation. Sometimes there is no traditional occupation that fits a person's talents and skills. Many people have become successful creating their own unique career.

Encourage your child's earliest inclinations. Sometimes they last a lifetime. Other times there is little connection, but keep track over the years. Provide your child information, visits to areas where occupational and vocational jobs are done, and encouragement to explore areas of interest, no matter how impossible it may appear to you.

Let your child know that the high school years are the best time to identify a calling, prepare to do it, and find a job doing it. You, the school counselor, or adults in the work world can help. So can books, getting out into the job scene to observe and participating through volunteer, part-time, or summer jobs. At least by the eleventh grade, have your teenager give serious time and thought to completing the next page. Having it completed during their senior year should make transition to work, job training, or college a smooth one.

Tell your teenager, "it is your job to figure out who you are, what you want from life, what you have to offer, where you want to go, and how you will get there. Aim at job satisfaction and development of your ability."

A Road Map to Reach Goals

Make a plan—a road map—of where you're going.

What you love to **do** (list the most liked first):

_____

_____

_____

Skills-What you do best (in order of the greatest skill first):

_____

_____

_____

Jobs that use those likes and skills (list your #1 preference first):	Years of Education Needed	Salary Range	
		Minimum	Maximum
1. _____	_____	_____	_____
2. _____	_____	_____	_____
3. _____	_____	_____	_____

Career exploration of those jobs-visits, people talked to, related jobs:

Place or Person	Phone #	Date	Email
_____	_____	_____	_____
_____	_____	_____	_____
_____	_____	_____	_____
_____	_____	_____	_____
_____	_____	_____	_____

Where education/training is available for first choice:

Date Visited	Entry Requirements	Date Application Submitted
1. _____	_____	_____
2. _____	_____	_____
3. _____	_____	_____

Immediate after-high-school job plans:

Job	Firm	Date Applied
_____	_____	_____
_____	_____	_____
_____	_____	_____

References you can use on job applications:

Name_____   Name_____

Street_____   Street_____

City_____State__Zip_____   City_____State__Zip_____

Phone #_____   Phone #_____

Email_____   Email_____

Make copies if additional space is needed.

Seventh Grade Developmental Record

Middle school is an exciting sometimes frightening experience. It is more "grown up," less childlike and more is expected. Be prepared, and help your child prepare to make this move smoothly.

Give more responsibilities and independence at home now, especially in managing time. Help your child be on time without your supervision, or work out a home study plan which includes an agreed-upon time when you do not interrupt and neither do friends.

Young people also become increasingly aware of their sexuality at this time. Teenage pregnancy continues to be a concern in our society. Boys and girls need help in coping with their new physical and emotional development. Help your child understand the broad implications of sexuality, fitting it into his or her developing identity with self-respect and respect for others. Talk about the responsibility that should be developed along with physical maturation.

Your child is perhaps also entering a new stage of mental ability. Logical thinking and abstract reasoning ability continue to develop. Continue to develop initiative through "doing" and staying positive. Have frequent "family times," doing things together and including your child's friends. Assign tasks that help your child become independent. Actively listen, especially to feelings. Encourage and support your child's interests.

Favorite School Subjects

1. _____
2. _____
3. _____

Friends:

1. _____
2. _____
3. _____

Talent or things well done:

1. _____
2. _____
3. _____

Loves best to do:

1. _____
2. _____
3. _____

Awards, honors and achievements:

1. _____
2. _____
3. _____

Areas of Concern:

1. _____
2. _____
3. _____

Area(s) where help is needed:

1. _____
2. _____
3. _____

Who will do what and when to help:
Teacher
_____

Parent
_____

Student
_____

Others
_____

Home/school responsibilities:

1. _____
2. _____
3. _____

Eighth Grade Developmental Record

The teenage years have arrived. Continue to:

- *Listen,* accepting feelings and ideas, even when they disagree with yours.
- Have frequent family time. Do enjoyable things together.
- Know your teen's friends.
- Maintain standards with clear limits. Expect those limits to be tested; be fair and reasonable, but firm.
- Encourage and support your teen's interests in constructive activities.

Abstract reasoning abilities should be developing and you can help your child:

- Consider all possibilities when solving a problem.
- Form as many solutions as possible.
- Think through the implications of each possible solution.
- Test each possibility against reality.

Routinely check the high school and district website. Your child may not bring home notes or notices about high school choices or course catalogs. Don't be afraid to call or email your child's guidance counselor to find out more. Get and read all of the information before the school year begins. Spend time talking with your teenager about goals, abilities, and interests in order to choose a good program and appropriate courses. See the guidance counselor when your child is asked to make course selections to discuss your ideas and ask any questions. Many districts have special programs such as IB (International Baccalaureate) or magnet programs (computers, engineering, and the arts). These special programs many times have special enrollment applications. Ask your guidance counselors if such programs exist and if so discuss with your child whether or not he/she would be interested. Check the district website for options and opportunities.

Favorite School Subjects:
1. _____
2. _____
3. _____

Friends:
1. _____
2. _____
3. _____

Talent or things well done:
1. _____
2. _____
3. _____

Loves best to do:
1. _____
2. _____
3. _____

Awards, honors and achievements:
1. _____
2. _____
3. _____

Colleges/Universities visited:
1. _____
2. _____
3. _____

Areas of Concern:
1. _____
2. _____
3. _____

Area(s) where help is needed:
1. _____
2. _____
3. _____

Who will do what and when to help:
Teacher
_____

Parent
_____

Student
_____

Others
_____

Jobs/Vocations explored:
1. _____
2. _____
3. _____

Ninth Grade Developmental Record

Your child is in high school. Communication sometimes breaks down as young people turn to their friends, especially if you have not built a firm foundation for communication. If there is trouble or misunderstanding, talk about it in reasonable tones. Use your teenager's developing reasoning skills for solving problems whenever possible.

Together:
- Consider all the possibilities available.
- Formulate as many solutions as possible.
- Think through the consequence of each solution.
- Test them against reality.

It is crucial now for there to be:
- "Family time" when you all share pleasant experiences.
- Knowledge of and inclusion of friends.
- Support for participation in constructive activities.
- Standards and limits—reasonable ones.
- Responsibilities valued by the family.
- An outside volunteer commitment.
- Active, sympathetic listening and understanding.

Encourage your child to participate in intramural sports or to develop their own physical fitness plan. Remember that the parents' role is to listen, support, clarify, and point out things students might not see.

Favorite School Subjects:
1.
2.
3.

Friends:
1.
2.
3.

Talent or things well done:
1.
2.
3.

Loves best to do:
1.
2.
3.

Awards, honors and achievements:
1.
2.
3.

Colleges/Universities visited:
1.
2.
3

Areas of Concern:
1.
2.
3.

Area(s) where help is needed:
1.
2.
3.

Who will do what and when to help:
Teacher

Parent

Student

Others

Jobs/Vocations explored:
1.
2.
3.

Home/School Responsibilities:
1.
2.
3.

Tenth Grade Developmental Record

Keep the team working together, but let your high school student take more of the lead each year. Love between parents and child leads to the child's independence and the development of a relationship of mutual respect. Help your teenage practice the adult skills of self-evaluation, decision-making, and assuming responsibility.

Maintain "family time," when all of you have quality time together. Family vacations, nightly dinners, family hikes or biking are all ways to spend quality family time. Active listening also becomes more important each year. Keep the communication channels open. Your experience and suggestions are valued, but may not always be welcomed while your child tries to "do things myself." Listen, ask questions, and help your child practice decision-making and self-correction.

From now on let your child ask and answer questions for the Yearly Educational Checkup, even if you still need to pose the questions and keep the record. Discuss with your teenager ideas about to how to accomplish goals. Provide experiences that help your teen explore and develop capacities.

Favorite School Subjects:
1. _____
2. _____
3. _____

Friends:
1. _____
2. _____
3. _____

Talent or things well done:
1. _____
2. _____
3. _____

Loves best to do:
1. _____
2. _____
3. _____

Awards, honors and achievements:
1. _____
2. _____
3. _____

Colleges/Universities visited:
1. _____
2. _____
3 _____

Areas of Concern:
1. _____
2. _____
3. _____

Area(s) where help is needed:
1. _____
2. _____
3. _____

Who will do what and when to help:
Teacher
_____

Parent
_____

Student
_____

Others
_____

Jobs/Vocations explored:
1. _____
2. _____
3. _____

Home/School Responsibilities:
1. _____
2. _____
3. _____

Eleventh Grade Developmental Record

This is the year to make important decisions. You and your child have been doing some of this exploration over the years. Continue to encourage your child to participate in school, church and community activities to develop skills, strengths and successes. Your child is probably spending more time with friends or on the computer, but continues to plan and encourage family activities. Continue listening and talking with your child about school, friends, jobs and activities.

Explore post-secondary vocations with your child. Is college right for him or her? If it is, what type of college would be appropriate? Plan time to visit different colleges and universities. If your child is not college bound try to find an apprenticeship in a career in which he/she is interested.

Make sure your child is on-track for graduation! The school guidance counselor can help with future planning whether it is a college choice or a vocational track.

Favorite School Subjects:
1. _____
2. _____
3. _____

Friends:
1. _____
2. _____
3. _____

Talent or things well done:
1. _____
2. _____
3. _____

Loves best to do:
1. _____
2. _____
3. _____

Awards, honors and achievements:
1. _____
2. _____
3. _____

Colleges/Universities visited:
1. _____
2. _____
3 _____

Areas of Concern:
1. _____
2. _____
3. _____

Area(s) where help is needed:
1. _____
2. _____
3. _____

Who will do what and when to help:
Teacher
_____

Parent
_____

Student
_____

Others
_____

Jobs/Vocations explored:
1. _____
2. _____
3. _____

Home/School Responsibilities:
1. _____
2. _____
3. _____

Twelfth Grade Developmental Record

Your child is a senior. Senioritis may set in—a breathing time, a plateau, a desire to relax and enjoy life. The momentum your child has developed will carry through if you have been doing your homework and your decision making in former years.

Maybe your child has a part-time job—hopefully one that pays off in more than money, i.e., in useful experience or opportunities for him or her to stretch, grow, and find out more about yourself.

Intimacy

Perhaps your child is entering or close to entering the next stage of emotional developmental, *intimacy.* Genuine intimacy is possible only after an identity has been established. *Intimacy* means caring unselfishly about another person, honestly and openly. Talk to your child about the seriousness of intimate relationships. Decisions made in the heat of the moment can last a lifetime.

Make sure your child is on-track for post-graduation. The guidance counselor can help your child with future planning whether it is a college choice or a vocational track. College applications need to be filled out and sent. Deposits need to be made. If your child is not going to college, set realistic goals as to when they have to have a job. Discuss what it means to be an adult and whether they will be financially responsible for room and board. If you don't want a child with the "failure to launch syndrome", you have to make sure he/she is ready for the real world.

Favorite School Subjects:
1. _____
2. _____
3. _____

Friends:
1. _____
2. _____
3. _____

Talent or things well done:
1. _____
2. _____
3. _____

Loves best to do:
1. _____
2. _____
3. _____

Awards, honors and achievements:
1. _____
2. _____
3. _____

Colleges/Universities visited:
1. _____
2. _____
3 _____

Areas of Concern:
1. _____
2. _____
3. _____

Area(s) where help is needed:
1. _____
2. _____
3. _____

Who will do what and when to help:
Teacher
_____

Parent
_____

Student
_____

Others
_____

Jobs/Vocations explored:
1. _____
2. _____
3. _____

Home/School Responsibilities:
1. _____
2. _____
3. _____

Part V
Computer Use, Summer Brain Drain, Resources, State Academic Standards, References

Parents Guide to the Internet and Computer Use

1. **Be involved and aware.** It is your job as a parent to teach your child about the Internet and computer use. Remember children imitate what we do. If you download music illegally they will too. Check out websites they visit. Most importantly talk about what is and is not appropriate.

2. **Talk to your children.** Ask them questions about where they're going online and who their buddies are. Explain to them that people are not always who they pretend to be.

3. **Stranger-Danger.** Teach about Internet danger. Identity theft and cyber stalking are real problems. Make sure they don't share personal information with anyone online. They should never post where they are going, telephone numbers, or anything else personal. Teach them about online "stranger danger". **Never** meet anyone in person that you've met online.

4. **Set rules.** Computers should be housed in an open area of your house. Set time limits and block sites that you deem inappropriate. Set time limits.

5. **Report suspicious activity.** If you feel your child is being bullied or stalked online report it to your Internet service provider or the National Center for Missing and Exploited Children (1-800-843-5678).

6. **Teach your child to spot fake or false information.** Just like the real world, everything you find online is not true. Teach them to be smart consumers of Internet information.

7. **Embrace their world.** Download music, IM your kids, play an online game, visit Facebook. Not only will your kids appreciate it, you'll know what you're dealing with!

Child and Teen Guide to Internet and Computer Use

1. **Know thy Neighbor.** Do not give out too much information online. Remember many sites are open to everyone. That means no last names, phone numbers (they can be used to track down your home), passwords, birth dates or years, or credit card information. Do not "friend" someone unless you know him or her. They could be a 50-year-old person posing as a teenager.

2. **Never meet up with anyone you don't already know.** 1 in 5 children and teens will be sexually solicited online. Don't post your schedule or say where you will be going. Don't make blanket statements about a party. If you don't want the world at your party, don't invite them.

3. **Don't fill out any "fun" questionnaires that are forwarded to you, even if they're from your friends.** Criminals and sex offenders use these to get personal information about you. Sometimes there is a ghost email that collects all the information.

4. **Stranger Danger.** Just like you wouldn't talk to random people on the street, make sure you know everyone on your buddy list. If you haven't met the people face-to-face, they may not be who they pretend to be.

5. **There's no such thing as "private" on the Internet.** You may think so, but it's not true. People can find anything they want—and keep what you post—forever.

6. **Be careful what you post:** Ask yourself would I want my mom, teacher, boss, or potential college advisor to see this? Pictures with identifiers, like where you go to school, can be shopping lists for online predators. Also if you pass along a sexy photo, you could be arrested for trafficking child pornography.

7. **Don't be a cyber bully.** Forwarding an embarrassing picture of someone else is a form of bullying. How would you like it if someone did that to you?

8. **Watch out for the worm.** Don't download content without your parents' permission. Many sites have spyware that will damage your computer. Other sites have really inappropriate content. Your parents can check your computer's URL history, so you can't hide where you've been. Downloading movies or music without paying for it is a crime.

9. **No Sharing.** I know that you were always told to share, but when it comes to your passwords **do not** give them to anyone but your parents. Your "friends" could post things or send things under your name and you would have no way of proving you didn't do it.

Internet by Age

The following age groups are approximate. Parents are encouraged to stay ahead of the Internet "learning curve".

Age 2 to 6: There are some great sites for children, but you must be right there to teach them how to use the computer and make sure the site is appropriate. Having your child sit on your lap and helping him/her navigate is a good idea. This is another way to spend 1-1 time with your child, however so will playing outside, reading a book, or listening to music.

Ages 7-9: Supervised independent use. Some kids will want to start emailing. This is absolutely fine, although IM isn't a good idea for this age group, as Instant Messaging (IM) buddies and buddy lists are too hard to monitor. They might want to start Web surfing. If they do, use a filter or tell them where they can go with your supervision. Most browsers have parental controls that block inappropriate sites. Don't let kids this age into chat rooms, play online games, **or download without you.**

Ages 10-12: Children will begin to explore on their own for school and for fun. "IM-ing" comes into play here for the first time—more so for girls than for boys. The boys are going to wander more on the Internet finding gaming sites and sites with silly and often inappropriate content. Some kids may start experimenting with MySpace and other social networks. Make sure you monitor their spaces. Insist on knowing his/her passwords and check the site often. Discuss with the child what is cyber bullying. If you wouldn't want it said about you or you wouldn't say it to their face, it isn't appropriate.

Ages 13-16: The floodgates open. Everything comes into play. It's entirely age-appropriate for this group to email, IM, surf the Web, download, and play games. But you have to make sure your kids know your rules. Also at this point, parents begin to lose control over where their kids use their computers. Trust comes into play.

17+: By now, if they don't know the rules of safe and responsible conduct on the Web, there's little we can do. Developmentally, teens are independent. But remind them that to stay safe, they need to keep personal information personal, and use their powers of critical thinking before they believe everything they see and read on the Web.

The Summer Brain Drain

One of the important causes of underachievement in our schools is children who are not involved in learning over the summer. Over twenty years of research prove that the summer leaning loss is real. The RAND Corporation and John Hopkins University found significant learning loss, particularly during the elementary school years. It was also found that this learning loss is cumulative, year after year, and has a . . . . "tremendous impact on students' success, including high school graduation, post secondary education, and work force preparedness".

This brain drain is preventable! Parents' involvement in their child's education should not stop during the summer months when schools are closed. Not only can parents prevent an achievement gap, they can help their child get ahead.

The following represents a few ideas for summer learning:

Consult with school before the summer recess. Ask for a summer reading list and any other suggestions the school can offer.

As a result of using this annual, you have collected information regarding your child's progress, or lack of progress. With the school's input, use this information to plan a learning program for the summer.

Attend summer school programs offered by the school or other organizations.

Make a schedule that blocks out time for learning.

Join a summer book club.

Visit museums.

Visit the library frequently.

Attend summer camps that have specific objectives (math, science, etc.)

Many worthwhile sites on the internet can help students during the summer, or any other time of the year. First and foremost, do your homework before using a particular site.

A Final Note

Again, it is not expected that you will do everything in this book. Select what is comfortable for you and your child. I hope I motivated you to take action because the rewards are enormous.

Your involvement will lead to: higher grades and test scores, improved educational experiences, improved emotional well-being, better classroom behavior, better social skills, improved school attendance.

Refer to this book frequently, use it as recommended, and enjoy your child(ren).

Best Wishes and "Welcome to the Faculty".

Bill Pelaia

State Academic Standards

Alabama
www.ade.state.az.us/standards/contentstandards.asp

Arkansas
www.arkansased.org/educators/curriculum/frameworks.html

California
www.cde.ca.gov/be/st/ss/index.asp

Colorado
www.cde.state.co.us/cdeassess/documents/OSA/k12_standards.html

Connecticut
www.sde.ct.gov/sde/cwp/view.asp?a=2618&Q=320954&sdenav_gid=1757

Delaware
www.doe.k12.de.us/infosuites/staff/ci/DRC/drc_contentStandards.shtml

District of Columbia
www.dcps.dc.gov/portal/site/DCPS/Teachingandlearning/Standards_by_Subject_Area.htm

Florida
www.floridastandards.org/downloads.aspx

Georgia
www.georgiastandards.org/Standards/Pages/BrowseStandards/BrowseGPS.aspx

Hawaii
www.standardstoolkit.k12.hi.us/index.html

Idaho
www.sde.idaho.gov/site/content_standards/

Illinois
www.isbe.state.il.us/ils/

Indiana
www.dc.doe.in.gov/Standards/AcademicStandards/index.shtml

Iowa
www.corecurriculum.iowa.gov/

Kansas

www.ksde.org/Default.aspx?tabid=1678

Kentucky
www.education.ky.gov/KDE/Instructional+Resources/Curriculum+Documents+and+Resources/Core+Content+for+Assessment/Core+Content+for+Assessment+4.1/

Louisiana
www.doe.state.la.us/lde/saa/1222.html

Maine
www.maine.gov/education/lres/

Maryland
www.mdk12.org/assessments/vsc/index.html

Massachusetts
www.doe.mass.edu/frameworks/

Michigan
www.michigan.gov/mde/0,1607,7-140-28753—,00.html

Minnesota
www.education.state.mn.us/MDE/Academic_Excellence/Academic_Standards/index.html

Mississippi
www.mde.k12.ms.us/Curriculum/index_1.htm

Missouri
www.dese.mo.gov/divimprove/curriculum/GLE/

Montana
www.opi.mt.gov/Curriculum/Index.html?gpm=1_8

Nebraska
www.education.ne.gov/ndestandards/AcademicStandards.htm

Nevada
www.doe.nv.gov/standards.html

New Hampshire
www.education.nh.gov/spotlight/k12_ccss.htm

New Jersey
www.state.nj.us/education/cccs/

New Mexico

www.ped.state.nm.us/nmStandards.html

New York
www.p12.nysed.gov/ciai/cores.html

North Dakota
www.dpi.state.nd.us/standard/content.shtm

North Carolina
www.ncpublicschools.org/curriculum/

Ohio
www.ode.state.oh.us/GD/Templates/Pages/ODE/ODEPrimary.aspx?Page=2&TopicID=1695&TopicRelationID=1696

Oklahoma
www.sde.state.ok.us/Curriculum/PASS/default.html

Oregon
www.ode.state.or.us/search/results/?id=53

Pennsylvania
www.pdesas.org/Standard/Views

Rhode Island
www.ride.ri.gov/Instruction/stand_frameworks_default.aspx

South Carolina
www.ed.sc.gov/agency/Standards-and-Learning/Academic-Standards/old/cso/

South Dakota
www.doe.sd.gov/contentstandards/index.asp

Tennessee
www.tennessee.gov/education/curriculum.shtml

Texas
www.tea.state.tx.us/index2.aspx?id=6148

Utah
www.uen.org/core/

Vermont
www.education.vermont.gov/new/html/pubs/framework.html

Virginia

www.doe.virginia.gov/testing/index.shtml

Washington
www.k12.wa.us/CurriculumInstruct/default.aspx

West Virginia
www.wvde.state.wv.us/policies/csos.html

Wisconsin
www.dpi.state.wi.us/standards/index.html

Wyoming
www.edu.wyoming.gov/Programs/standards.aspx

Organizational Resources

American Homeschool Association

www.americanhomeschoolassociation.org/

The American Homeschool Association has been serving homeschooling families with advocacy, support, information and networking since 1995. The AHA supports, encourages and promotes all approaches to bona fide homeschooling.

Council for Exceptional Children

www.cec.sped.org//AM/Template.cfm?Section=Home

2900 Crystal Drive,
Suite 1000
Arlington, VA 22202-2557

The Council for Exceptional Children (CEC) works to improve the educational success of individuals with disabilities and/or gifts and talents.

Federal Student Aid

www.studentaid.ed.gov/PORTALSWebApp/students/english/aboutus.jsp

Federal Student Aid, an office of the U.S. Department of Education, plays a central and essential role in America's postsecondary education community. Our core mission is to ensure that all eligible individuals benefit from federal financial assistance—grants, loans and work-study programs—for education beyond high school. The Federal Student Aid team is passionately committed to making education beyond high school more attainable for all Americans, regardless of socioeconomic status. By championing access to postsecondary education, we uphold its value as a force for greater inclusion in American society and for the continued vitality of America as a nation.

Homeschool.com

www.homeschool.com/

Homeschool.com helps homeschooling families get the information they need about the different curriculum, products and services offered to the homeschooling community.

National Association for the Education of Young Children

www.naeyc.org/

1313 L Street, NW, Suite 500
Washington, DC 20005

The National Association for the Education of Young Children (NAEYC) is dedicated to improving the well-being of all young children, with particular focus on the quality of educational and developmental services for all children from birth through age 8. NAEYC is committed to becoming an increasingly high performing and inclusive organization.

National Coalition for Parent Involvement in Education

www.ncpie.org/AboutNCPIE/

National Coalition for Parent Involvement in Education (NCPIE)
1400 L Street NW, Suite 300
Washington DC 20005

The National Coalition for Parent Involvement in Education advocates the involvement of parents and families in their children's education, and fosters relationships between home, school, and community to enhance the education of all young people.

National Education Association

www.nea.org/parents

National Education Association
1201 16th Street, NW
Washington, DC 20036-3290

The National Education Association has developed guides to provide parents and caregivers with fundamental tools to encourage their children's success in school.

National Joint Committee on Learning Disabilities

www.ldonline.org/about/partners/njcld

2775 S. Quincy St.
Arlington, VA 22206

Founded in 1975, the National Joint Committee on Learning Disabilities (NJCLD) is a national committee of representatives of organizations committed to the education and welfare of individuals with learning disabilities. More than 350,000 individuals constitute the membership of the organizations represented by the NJCLD.

National Parent Teacher Association

www.pta.org/

National PTA Headquarters
1250 N. Pitt Street
Alexandria, Virginia 22314

As the largest volunteer child advocacy association in the nation, National Parent Teacher Association (PTA) provides parents and families with a powerful voice to speak on behalf of every child and the best tools to help their children be safe, healthy, and successful—in school and in life.

National Society for the Gifted & Talented

www.nsgt.org/

River Plaza
9 West Broad Street
Stamford, CT 06902-3788

The National Society for the Gifted & Talented™ (NSGT) is a not-for-profit 501(c)(3) organization created to honor and encourage gifted and talented (G&T) children and youth. It is committed to acknowledging and supporting the needs of these children and youth by providing recognition of their significant academic and artistic accomplishments and access to educational resources and advanced learning opportunities directly related to their interests and talent areas.

National Youth Leadership Council

www.nylc.org/

1667 Snelling Avenue North, Suite D300
Saint Paul, Minnesota 55108

For more than two decades, National Youth Leadership Council has led a movement linking youths, educators, and communities to redefine the roles of young people in society.

Parent Involvement Matters

www.parentinvolvementmatters.org/

National ParentNet Association
P.O. Box 11609
Bainbridge, WA 98110

Parent Involvement Matters is committed to increasing parent involvement in all forms and to sharing resources between the many groups and organizations working toward the goal of developing parent-school-community partnerships that help kids thrive.

The Partnership at Drugfree.org

www.drugfree.org/

352 Park Avenue South
9th Floor
New York, NY 10010

The Partnership at Drugfree.org is a nonprofit organization that helps parents prevent, intervene in and find treatment for drug and alcohol use by their children.

Project Appleseed

www.projectappleseed.org/

Project Appleseed

520 Melville Avenue
St. Louis, MO 63130-4506

Project Appleseed is a nonprofit resource and advocate for families engaged in education

and the pursuit of life, liberty and happiness in America's public schools.

References

Bloom, Benjamin. (1976). *Human characteristics and school learning.* New York: McGraw-Hill. Written for educators about mastery learning, but parents may be interested in knowing that most students' learning is enhanced when there are favorable learning conditions. A description of these conditions is given.

Ellis, Albert. (1966). *How to raise an emotionally healthy, happy child.* Los Angeles: Whilshire Book Company. Chapters deal with helping children with fears and anxieties, problems of achievement, hospitality, sex problems, conduct problems, and personal behavior problems.

Erikson, Erik. (1963). *Childhood and society.* New York: W.W. Norton. The classic work in explaining psychosocial developmental stages. This is a basis for many of the tasks suggested in this manual.

Gesell, A., & Amabruda, C.S. (1947). *Developmental diagnosis: Normal and abnormal child development.* New York: Harper & Row. A basic description of child development.
Havighurst, R.J. (1972). *Developmental tasks and education (3rd ed).* New York: David McKay. An inventory of tasks by age.

Henderson, A. T., Johnson, V. R., Mapp, K. L., & Davies, D. (2007). *Beyond the bake sale: The essential guide to family/school partnerships.* New York: The New Press. A guide to developing positive family, school, and community partnerships.

Holt, John. (1981). *Teach your own.* New York: Delacorate Press. Holt is the leader in home schooling. This book will discuss how you can better work with the schools, or in a home schooling network.

Kohlberg, Lawrence. (1969). *Stages in the development of moral thought and action.* New York: Holt, Rinehart & Winston. Kohlberg is the leading authority in moral development.

Maslow, Abraham (1970). *Motivation and personality.* New York: Harper and Row. This work examines basic needs that a child needs to grow and learn.

Piaget, Jean (1952). *The origins of intelligence in children.* New York: Basic Books. This book describes the stages of cognitive development in young children to adults.

Sax, Leonard (2005). *Why gender matters: What parents and teachers need to know about the emerging science of sex differences.* New York: Doubleday. This book examines the science of sex differences.

Sweeney, Michael (2009). *Brain: The complete mind: How it develops, how it works, and how to keep it sharp.* New York: Random House. A guide to the brain's development and function.

Part VI
Educational Records

Preschool-Grade 12

For every grade save the following information:
Report Cards
Class Schedules
School Policies
Notes and emails from School
Copies of Notes and emails to School
Rules and Regulations
School Handbook
School Calendar
Bus routes and Schedules
PTA Information
School Advisory Information
Tests
Medical Check-ups
Samples of School Work
Photo

Pre-School Educational Record

School _____ Principal _____

School phone number _____ Counselor _____

School address _____ Zip _____

Daily time
schedule: From _____ to _____ Lunch from _____ to _____

Daily bus schedule:
Picked up _____ Returned home _____

Room number _____ Teacher _____ Email _____

**Important
Dates** Appointment to see school records _____ Yearly educational check-up conference _____

Report cards sent home _____ _____ _____ _____

Teacher conferences schedule

_____ _____ _____ _____

Photo	Dates	Standardized tests and results
	_____	_____
	_____	_____
		Reasons child missed school
	_____	_____
	_____	_____
	_____	_____
	_____	_____
	_____	_____

Check your list with the school's record given on report card.

School Year _____

Kindergarten Educational Record

School _____ Principal _____

School phone number _____ Counselor _____

School address _____ Zip _____

Daily time
schedule: From _____ to _____ Lunch from _____ to _____

Daily bus schedule:
Picked up _____ Returned home _____

Room number _____ Teacher _____ Email _____

**Important
Dates**

Appointment to see school records _____ Yearly educational check-up conference _____

Report cards sent home _____ _____ _____ _____

Teacher conferences schedule

_____ _____ _____

Photo	Dates	Standardized tests and results
	_____	_____
	_____	_____
		Reasons child missed school
	_____	_____
	_____	_____
	_____	_____
	_____	_____

Check your list with the school's record given on report card.

School Year _____

First-Grade Educational Record

School _____ Principal _____

School phone number _____ Counselor _____

School address _____ Zip _____

Daily time
schedule: From _____ to _____ Lunch from _____ to _____

Daily bus schedule:
Picked up _____ Returned home _____

Room number _____ Teacher _____ Email _____

**Important
Dates** Appointment to see school records _____ Yearly educational check-up conference _____

Report cards sent home _____ _____ _____ _____

Teacher conferences schedule

_____ _____ _____

	Dates	Standardized tests and results
Photo	_____	_____
	_____	_____
		Reasons child missed school
	_____	_____
	_____	_____
	_____	_____
	_____	_____
	_____	_____

Check your list with the school's record given on report card.

School Year _____

Second-Grade Educational Record

School _____ Principal _____

School phone number _____ Counselor _____

School address _____ Zip _____

Daily time
schedule: From _____ to _____ Lunch from _____ to _____

Daily bus schedule:
Picked up _____ Returned home _____

Room number _____ Teacher _____ Email _____

**Important
Dates**

Appointment to see school records _____ Yearly educational check-up conference _____

Report cards sent home _____ _____ _____ _____

Teacher conferences schedule

_____ _____ _____

Photo	Dates	Standardized tests and results

Dates   Standardized tests and results

_____ _____

_____ _____

Reasons child missed school

_____ _____

_____ _____

_____ _____

_____ _____

_____ _____

Check your list with the school's record given on report card.

School Year _____

Third-Grade Educational Record

School _____ Principal _____

School phone number _____ Counselor _____

School address _____ Zip _____

Daily time
schedule: From _____ to _____ Lunch from _____ to _____

Daily bus schedule:
Picked up _____ Returned home _____

Room number _____ Teacher _____ Email _____

**Important
Dates**   Appointment to see school records _____ Yearly educational check-up conference _____

Report cards sent home _____ _____ _____ _____

Teacher conferences schedule

_____   _____   _____

Photo	Dates	Standardized tests and results
	_____	_____
	_____	_____
		Reasons child missed school
	_____	_____
	_____	_____
	_____	_____
	_____	_____
	_____	Check your list with the school's record given on report card.

School Year _____

Fourth-Grade Educational Record

School _____ Principal _____

School phone number _____ Counselor _____

School address _____ Zip _____

Daily time
schedule: From _____ to _____ Lunch from _____ to _____

Daily bus schedule:
Picked up _____ Returned home _____

Room number _____ Teacher _____ Email _____

**Important
Dates**
Appointment to see school records _____ Yearly educational check-up conference _____

Report cards sent home _____ _____ _____ _____

Teacher conferences schedule

_____   _____

Photo	Dates	Standardized tests and results
	_____	_____
	_____	_____
		Reasons child missed school
	_____	_____
	_____	_____
	_____	_____
	_____	_____
	_____	_____

Check your list with the school's record given on report card.

School Year _____

Fifth-Grade Educational Record

School _____ Principal _____

School phone number _____ Counselor _____

School address _____ Zip _____

Daily time
schedule: From _____ to _____ Lunch from _____ to _____

Daily bus schedule:
Picked up _____ Returned home _____

Room number _____ Teacher _____ Email _____

**Important
Dates** Appointment to see school records _____ Yearly educational check-up conference _____

Report cards sent home _____ _____ _____ _____

Teacher conferences schedule

_____ _____ _____

	Dates	Standardized tests and results
	_____	_____
	_____	_____

Reasons child missed school

Photo

_____ _____

_____ _____

_____ _____

_____ _____

_____ Check your list with the school's record given on report card.

School Year _____

Sixth-Grade Educational Record

School _____ Principal _____

School phone number _____ Counselor _____

School address _____ Zip _____

Daily time
schedule: From _____ to _____ Lunch from _____ to _____

Daily bus schedule:
Picked up _____ Returned home _____

Room number _____ Teacher _____ Email _____

**Important
Dates**   Appointment to see school records _____ Yearly educational check-up conference _____

Report cards sent home _____   _____   _____   _____

Teacher conferences schedule

_____   _____   _____

	Dates	Standardized tests and results
	_____	_____
	_____	_____
Photo		**Reasons child missed school**
	_____	_____
	_____	_____
	_____	_____
	_____	_____
	_____	Check your list with the school's record given on report card.

School Year _____

Seventh-Grade Educational Record

School _____ Principal _____

School phone number _____ Counselor _____

School address _____ Zip _____

Daily time
schedule: From _____ to _____ Lunch from _____ to _____

Daily bus schedule:
Picked up _____ Returned home _____

Room number _____ Teacher _____ Email _____

**Important
Dates**   Appointment to see school records _____ Yearly educational check-up conference _____

Report cards sent home _____ _____ _____ _____

Teacher conferences schedule

_____ _____ _____

	Dates	Standardized tests and results

Photo

School Year _____

Reasons child missed school

Check your list with the school's record given on report card.

Eighth-Grade Educational Record

School _____ Principal _____

School phone number _____ Counselor _____

School address _____ Zip _____

Daily time
schedule: From _____ to _____ Lunch from _____ to _____

Daily bus schedule:
Picked up _____ Returned home _____

Room number _____ Teacher _____ Email _____

**Important
Dates** Appointment to see school records _____ Yearly educational check-up conference _____

Report cards sent home _____ _____ _____ _____

Teacher conferences schedule

_____ _____

Photo	Dates	Standardized tests and results
	_____	_____
	_____	_____
		Reasons child missed school
	_____	_____
	_____	_____
	_____	_____
	_____	_____
	_____	Check your list with the school's record given on report card.

School Year _____

Ninth-Grade Educational Record

School _____ Principal _____

School phone number _____ Counselor _____

School address _____ Zip _____

Daily time
schedule: From _____ to _____ Lunch from _____ to _____

Daily bus schedule:
Picked up _____ Returned home _____

Room number _____ Teacher _____ Email _____

**Important
Dates**   Appointment to see school records _____ Yearly educational check-up conference _____

Report cards sent home _____ _____ _____ _____

Teacher conferences schedule

_____ _____ _____

<table>
<tr><td rowspan="10">Photo</td><td>Dates</td><td>Standardized tests and results</td></tr>
<tr><td>_____</td><td>_____</td></tr>
<tr><td>_____</td><td>_____</td></tr>
<tr><td></td><td>Reasons child missed school</td></tr>
<tr><td>_____</td><td>_____</td></tr>
<tr><td>_____</td><td>_____</td></tr>
<tr><td>_____</td><td>_____</td></tr>
<tr><td>_____</td><td>_____</td></tr>
<tr><td>_____</td><td>_____</td></tr>
<tr><td>_____</td><td>Check your list with the school's record given on report card.</td></tr>
</table>

School Year _____

Tenth-Grade Educational Record

School _____ Principal _____

School phone number _____ Counselor _____

School address _____ Zip _____

Daily time
schedule: From _____ to _____ Lunch from _____ to _____

Daily bus schedule:
Picked up _____ Returned home _____

Room number _____ Teacher _____ Email _____

**Important
Dates**   Appointment to see school records _____ Yearly educational check-up conference _____

Report cards sent home _____ _____ _____ _____

Teacher conferences schedule

_____   _____   _____

Photo	Dates	Standardized tests and results
	_____	_____
	_____	_____
		Reasons child missed school
	_____	_____
	_____	_____
	_____	_____
	_____	_____
	_____	

Check your list with the school's record given on report card.

School Year _____

Eleventh-Grade Educational Record

School _____ Principal _____

School phone number _____ Counselor _____

School address _____ Zip _____

Daily time
schedule: From _____ to _____ Lunch from _____ to _____

Daily bus schedule:
Picked up _____ Returned home _____

Room number _____ Teacher _____ Email _____

**Important
Dates**   Appointment to see school records _____ Yearly educational check-up conference _____

Report cards sent home _____ _____ _____ _____

Teacher conferences schedule

_____ _____ _____

Photo	Dates	Standardized tests and results
	_____	_____
	_____	_____
		Reasons child missed school
	_____	_____
	_____	_____
	_____	_____
	_____	_____
	_____	_____

Check your list with the school's record given on report card.

School Year _____

Twelfth-Grade Educational Record

School _____ Principal _____

School phone number _____ Counselor _____

School address _____ Zip _____

Daily time
schedule: From _____ to _____ Lunch from _____ to _____

Daily bus schedule:
Picked up _____ Returned home _____

Room number _____ Teacher _____ Email _____

**Important
Dates**   Appointment to see school records _____ Yearly educational check-up conference _____

Report cards sent home _____ _____ _____ _____

Teacher conferences schedule

_____   _____   _____

	Dates	Standardized tests and results
	_____	_____
	_____	_____

Photo

Reasons child missed school

_____ _____

_____ _____

_____ _____

_____ _____

_____ Check your list with the school's record given on report card.

School Year _____